Sand, Sea, and Sky

Sand, Sea, and Sky: My Love Affair with Tahiti

I have tried to recreate events, locales, and conversations from my memories of them. Some names and identifying details have been changed to protect the privacy of individuals.

To connect with Carol, you can reach her at sandseaandskybook@gmail.com

Library of Congress Control Number: 2024909554

CPSIA Code: PRV0724A

ISBN-13: 979-8-89138-119-3

Printed in the United States

Author photo credit: Sarah Lee
Cover design contribution: Ron Haake

It is with a full heart that I acknowledge my husband, Scooter, also known as "Scott" and "Scotch" on the atoll. He has been by my side as we have built a life together in our beloved shack in the sand. He is the yin to my yang, the Desi to my Lucy, and the man who rarely questions my sanity when, in fact, he should. He has been one half of the team as we have navigated a life much different from what either of us had known before.

It is with a heavy heart that I acknowledge my parents, Roy and Marjorie Roberts. They introduced me to the magic of Tahiti way back in my growing-up days. Not a day passes that I don't think of them. I would give anything to have them join us here on our lanai. We'd listen to the good old Tahitian music, have a sip of rum, and watch the parade of canoes and sailboats pass by out front.

It is with a thankful and humble heart that I acknowledge the people of Rangiroa, who have welcomed us with open arms. Specifically, thanks to Scarlett and Rich and Teiva and Meho. Without their help, nonc of this would have been possible.

A MEMOIR BY **Carol Fuller**

Sand, Sea, and Sky

My Love Affair with Tahiti

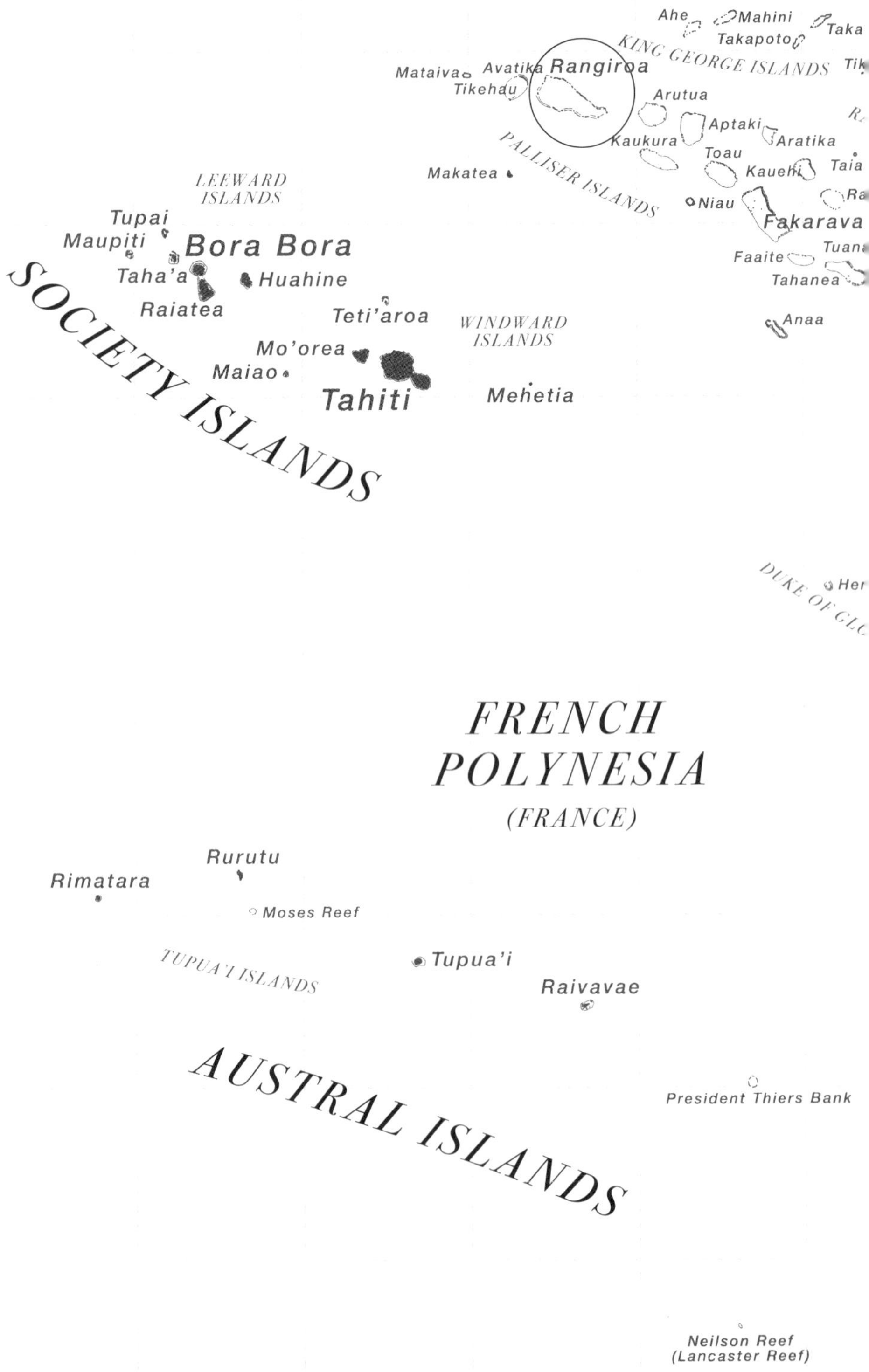
Ahe
Mahini
Takapoto
KING GEORGE ISLANDS
Mataiva
Avatika
Rangiroa
Tikehau
Arutua
Aptaki
Aratika
Kaukura
Toau
Taia
Makatea
PALLISER ISLANDS
Kauehi
Niau
Fakarava
Faaite
Tahanea
Anaa
LEEWARD ISLANDS
Tupai
Maupiti
Bora Bora
Taha'a
Huahine
Raiatea
SOCIETY ISLANDS
Teti'aroa
WINDWARD ISLANDS
Mo'orea
Maiao
Tahiti
Mehetia
FRENCH POLYNESIA
(FRANCE)
Rurutu
Rimatara
Moses Reef
TUPUA'I ISLANDS
Tupua'i
Raivavae
AUSTRAL ISLANDS
President Thiers Bank
Neilson Reef
(Lancaster Reef)

Tepoto (North)
Napuka
DISAPPOINTMENT ISLANDS
Puka-Puka
TUAMOTU ARCHIPELAGO
Takume
Fangatau
Fakahina
Raroia
Nihiru
Rekareka (Tehuata)
Marutea Nord
Tatakoto
Tekokota
Tauere
Hikueru
HIKUERU GROUP
Amanu
Marokau
Ravahere
Hao
Pukarua
Reao
HAO GROUP
Akiaki
Nengonengo
Vahitahi
Manuhangi
Paraoa
Nukutavake
Vairaatea
Pinaki
Ahunui
FAR EAST TUAMOTU GROUP
Nukutepipi
Vanavana
Tureia
Tenararo
Vahanga
Tenarunga
Marutea Atoll
Matureivavao
Tematagi
Moruroa
ACTEON GROUP
Maria Atoll
Fangataufa
SOUTH PACIFIC OCEAN
N
NE
E
SE
S
SW
W
NW

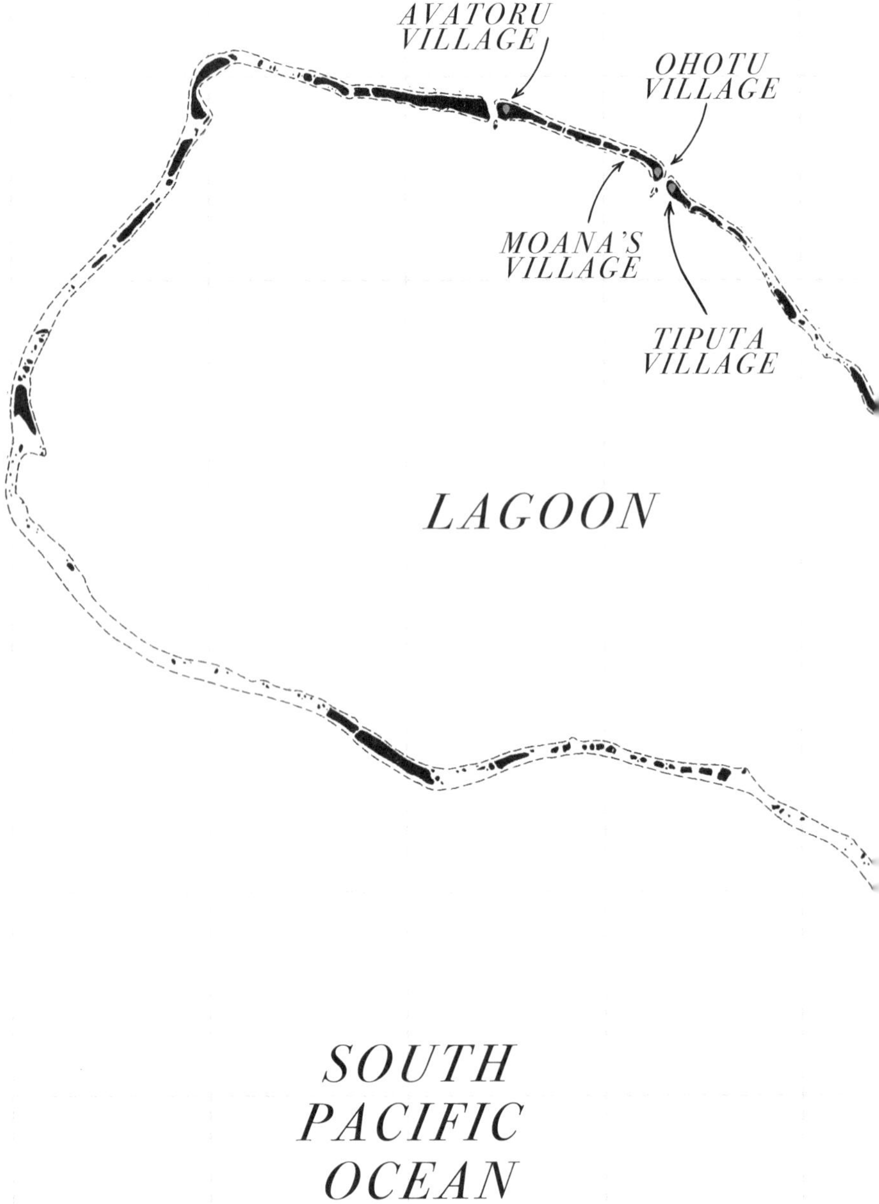
AVATORU VILLAGE
OHOTU VILLAGE
MOANA'S VILLAGE
TIPUTA VILLAGE
LAGOON
SOUTH PACIFIC OCEAN

RANGIROA
SOUTH PACIFIC OCEAN
N
NE
E
SE
S
SW
W
NW

COMMUNITY TIARE GARDEN
Avatoru Village
MOANA'S VILLAGE
Walkway to Beach
William's fare pote'e
LAGOON

SOUTH PACIFIC OCEAN
REEF BEACH
Ohotu Village
François & Jeanne
Joa Charlie Noam & Tara
COCONUT FOREST
Fare Fuller
N
NE
E
SE
S
SW
W
NW
BEACH

INTRODUCTION

We are settled comfortably in seats 14A and 14B. This is Hawaiian Airlines Flight 481 bound for Pape'ete from Honolulu. As always, the flight is electrified with excitement. Many passengers appear to be honeymooners. Others are Tahitians loaded down with overflowing bags after a week-long shopping spree in Waikiki. A large group of passengers consists of members of a Hawaiian dance troupe. They have boarded the flight with fragile ukuleles, small drums, and jingle-jangling dance implements. There are several retired couples seated around us. Most of these retirees are taking a ten-day cruise through French Polynesia. They will check this item off their bucket list, then continue to other destinations next year. There is a smattering of others: surfers looking for pristine waves, single people looking for romance, and travelers looking for adventure. Then, there's us.

I'm hoping our four bags have made the connection from Kona. For three months, we have meticulously collected a vast array of goods. We have carefully packed this all up with practiced precision. Each bag is packed to exactly fifty-one pounds. We found out that Hawaiian Airlines lets that one-pound overage slide, and we use that extra pound per bag every trip. Our four carry-on bags, stuffed to capacity, probably total at least 100 more pounds. We will need to maneuver these eight pieces of luggage totaling 304 pounds for thirty hours until we reach the front door of our shack in the sand on Sunday at three in the afternoon.

As the crow flies, Kona is not that far from Rangiroa. Our three flights go north to Honolulu; south to Pape'ete; and then, after an overnight in Pape'ete, we backtrack north again on Air Tahiti to Rangiroa. The flights out to the Tuamotus are usually milk runs, making stops to at least one other atoll on the way. It's a zigzag trip that, if we think about it, is frustrating. That's just the way it is. We make this trek twice every year. We have learned to get in our extra comfort seats, relax, and just let things flow. Knowing that we will spend the next three months on the atoll make the hassle worth it. It will be a nice long stretch on "Tahitian Time" until we reverse the zigzagging and return to Kona with eight empty pieces of luggage.

Fellow passengers walking up and down the center aisle may take a casual look at us and think that we are embarking on the standard two-week Tahitian getaway. We are, in fact, part-time residents of Rangiroa, spending half of every year on the atoll. We are on Flight 481, heading home to a life we have worked long and hard to build.

My story began in Southern California more than sixty years ago. My childhood suburban home was fairly normal, with one big exception: we were immersed in all things Tahitian. My parents were the exuberant conduits. As a child, I whipped through my weekly chores to the beat of the *to'ere* drums pounding on Dad's hi-fi. I sang along with endless Tahitian LPs that magically drew me in, even though I didn't understand the lyrics. I met real Tahitians at huge backyard parties called *tama'ara'as,* and I watched the throng of partiers dance the *tamure* with wild abandon. I gazed incessantly at books, magazines, and photos of the South Seas, going back and forth, back and forth, endlessly studying each page and every minute detail of a place I could only dream about at that stage of my life. I quietly caressed the exotic shells that filled the family *tanoa* bowl. They were so enchanting to me. They were tangible objects that I could hold in my small hand from a place I was slowly beginning to idolize. It was during that time that I swallowed the lure—the lure of Tahiti. My course was set at the age of twelve.

As an adult, I picked up the baton from my mom and dad and began my own solo wanderings throughout all of French Polynesia. On that first trip, just off the plane, I inhaled the sweet fragrances, looked up at the southern stars, then kneeled down to touch the ground. I had finally made it. I had arrived at my long dreamed of home.

My story ends, as it should, with my husband and I finding

our special place on the coral atoll of Rangiroa. The following collection of stories tells how we found our way to our shack in the sand. The stories open a window into our day-to-day lives in a world vastly different from what we left behind. There have been ups and downs, lessons learned, the helping hands of many friends, a little heartbreak every now and then, and a lot of magic along the way. This is a story of living on a tropical island that many may dream of but few attempt. For me, it simply was not an option.

Carol C. Fuller

KONA 2023

Part One

Just like our zigzag flight plan from Kona to Rangiroa, this story will go back to where it all began before arriving at where we are today. Going back to my childhood will put things into perspective and explain why living on a coral atoll in French Polynesia made perfect sense.

TWO TAHITIAN HATS

Growing up in the 1950s and 1960s in Orange County, California, was a little like living on the set of *Leave It to Beaver*. Sure, things weren't as perfect inside every household as they were in the Cleaver's TV home. However, it was a perfect time and place to be a kid. It was midcentury Americana at its finest.

We were living in Downey, California, close to my dad's job at North American Aviation. I was just an infant at the time. Brice, my older brother, was about three. After camping out in our little rental house for a year, Mom and Dad set out to find a place to call their own. Dad picked up a compass and a map. He placed the point of that compass precisely on his work site at North American Aviation. Next, he inscribed a circle. The penciled circle he drew separated all of Southern California into two groups: neighborhoods that were within a thirty-minute driving distance of his office, and those that were not. Anything within that circle "made the cut." Next, all the places within his desired drive time were segregated once again: those that had Dad driving into the sun in the morning and then again in the evening as the sun set, and those that had him driving with his back to the rising and setting sun. After these variables had been shuffled about, my parents pinpointed their ideal location: Fullerton, in the middle of Orange County. It was close enough to work, and my dad could drive both ways while avoiding the glaring Southern California sun.

Dad and Mom found a piece of raw land. The parcel was a part of a gigantic orange grove. As much of the remaining orchard land was in the early 1950s in Southern California, the grove had been subdivided to make room for the postwar building boom. A few other homes had recently sprouted up along the pepper tree–lined street. All of them were very nice. Some of the neighboring houses were more established, and others could even be considered small ranches. There was a thoroughbred ranch right next to a Shetland pony ranch a few minutes walk up the street. There were no sidewalks, just a dusty dirt path along the roadsides where people rode their horses. One neighbor had an antique buggy collection. He'd hitch up his horses to a buckwagon, an old stagecoach, or an ominous hearse and clip-clop past, raising a cloud of dust behind him. Close by was a small lake, and even closer was a big, old country store with hitching posts out front. Valencia Mesa Drive, our street, was the last road. After that, it became wide-open country for miles. The neighborhood was called, appropriately, Sunny Hills.

Dad possessed a unique combination of genes. He was as precise, methodical, and technical as any aerospace engineer could be, these genes compliments of his engineer father. He inherited his artistic genes from his mother, the very first woman admitted to the prestigious Rhode Island School of Design on the merits of her charcoal drawings. These two diametrically opposed traits, creativity and calculation, served him well throughout his life. The pinnacle of his many projects was the house he built for his family there amid the orange groves.

Dad worked up some "contemporary ranch house" plans. Then, wearing an oversized straw hat, he cleared the land at the wheel of a red, bouncing tractor. He was careful to leave as many orange trees as possible, carving out just enough room for the house pad. He used hand-me-down tools from his dad's machine shop. Every weekend and after work, he was there working. He'd work on and on until the sky went black. He lorded over every detail, be it the paint, kitchen cabinetry, or the split rail fence out front. Yes, he had some help, but I think of that house as something Dad created out of sheer willpower, sweat, and determination.

Mom was the interior designer. She had an eye for fabrics, style, and quality, traits she inherited from her mother. Mom was also a decent gardener, thanks to her dad, who had a real way with propagating bromeliads and other exotic plants. Mom eventually created her pride and joy: two circular rose gardens out in the front yard.

Soon after we settled into our new home, my sister, Stephanie, joined the family. My parents eventually ended up spacing out us kids at exactly three-year intervals. The three-year interval between the Roberts kids had us at totally different stages of development. Just that fact alone must have made for overstressed parents, running ragged every which way. In addition, the social pressure placed on parents at that time was immense. Moms had to have their children dressed and groomed to unrealistic standards, while they created and maintained model homes and yards, attended charity groups and school functions, and looked like Doris Day in a starched gingham apron while doing all of it. Dads left each morning for a job in a nice, shiny car. They wore a freshly pressed white shirt under a suit and tie and usually carried a black lunch box. They didn't return home until six in the evening. At that time, the cocktail whistle went off, and parents fortified themselves liberally for the next day that would be exactly the same.

There were hundreds of kids all over Sunny Hills. We were baby boomers. Most of us there lived with a mom and a dad in an upper-middle-class home set along rambling country streets with names like Rodeo Road and Lakeview.

All of us ran wild all summer long. We would leave the house at dawn and only come home when we heard Dad's piercing whistle, signifying dinner time. There might have been a pit stop during the day for a slapped-together bologna sandwich and a gulp from the garden hose, but other than that, we were on our own. There were acres of orange and avocado trees. We set up camps and forts in the groves and had fights with ripe fruit against warring bands of hooligans. There was a loose network of well-worn, dusty trails to hike, bike, and ride horses on. The trails meandered around stands of tall eucalyptus trees, a lush oasis-like lake, and countless carefully organized rows of orange and avocado trees. Occasionally, we'd spot a rattlesnake, a jack rabbit, or a roadrunner during our explorations. A few different railroad tracks crisscrossed the hills and gulches and wound under narrow bridges.

The Sunny Hills kids ruled these wild trails. We'd ride bikes in packs all day and into the evening. We built rudimentary skateboards using cannibalized roller skates and two-by-fours. There was a swimming club, Jimmy Smith's. It had four pools and a popcorn machine. I was on a swimming or diving team almost every summer of my life up until the end of high school. Also in the mix was the Big Red Barn, a gathering place for kids and adults for all types of activities. It had a huge, squeaky, white oak dance floor with a ring of antique wagons and buggies around the perimeter. There was a little café just off to one side in a corner of the barn called The Chuckwagon. I learned to square dance in the barn with my Girl Scout troop and tasted Thousand Island dressing for the first time in my life at that café.

Just behind the Big Red Barn was the rodeo ring. Weekly competitions were held, and judges handed out well-earned ribbons. I'd ride in Western events and later got into English riding. We had a loose-knit gang of riders, mostly girls. We called ourselves the Ranch Town Riders. All-day rides to the far end of the hills would find us coming upon dark-haired herdsmen in little wagons tending flocks of goats and sheep. Come the end of summer, we all buckled down and went to school. We were good students, and we followed the rules. If we didn't, we all knew the consequences: Our parents had no reservations about the heavy and serious discipline administered by Dad when he got home from what we called the salt mines.

One warm summer day, our family went over to a friend's house for a swim. The Barkers were rich. Even at age six, I could tell. Their home was impressive. They had a neat gravel driveway in the shape of a half circle leading up to their front door. In the backyard, they had a pool. Behind the pool was an immaculate stable housing Valerie Barker's spirited Arabian horse. There was more: a small cabana adjacent to the pool. Dad called it a "change booth." I had never seen one before. Naturally, we kids were let loose to do what we wanted. And what we wanted was to play and scream like banshees in the pool. The adults retreated to the darkened patio. They tucked themselves in around the cocktail cart, smoked long, thin filter-tipped cigarettes, and proceeded to party the afternoon away.

After my skin pruned up from too long in the Barkers' pool, I wrapped a towel around my waist and took myself on a self-guided tour of the change booth. I was fascinated by such a tiny structure. Inside I saw two doors. Each door had a sign above it and a woven hat. I was just learning to read at school. The two words didn't make sense to me. I trudged over to get my dad for some help. Inside that tiny change booth, I got my very first Tahitian lesson. *TANE*, Dad said, meant "man" in Tahitian. The hat up there is a man's hat made from a palm frond. The word *VAHINE*, he continued, meant "woman" in Tahitian; that palm-frond hat was made for a woman. Dad helped me compare the hat styles. The man's hat was tall, angular, and crisp. The woman's hat was flowing, curvy, and low. He continued to tell me that these hats were from a very special and magical place, a place that he wanted to go . . . Tahiti.

I had long forgotten about that day with Dad and the two Tahitian hats. The memory recently came flooding back to me in the sharpest of details. Looking back at this memory from here and now, it makes me wonder, and yet it makes perfect sense. That little shared moment with my dad and just the thought of a magical place called Tahiti was the beginning. As it turned out, Tahiti would become our common denominator, our shared passion. As the years passed, he and I both continued in our own respective time and our own respective ways to chase, and to capture, that magnificent Tahitian magic.

— POSTSCRIPT —

Dad's gone now. The house on Valencia Mesa is still there, looking as beautiful as ever. Over the years, it has gone through several additions, remodels, and occupants. Dad's vision is still abundantly evident. There is something else there now as well. The kind family currently calling it home planted a tree just out by the front door. In the soil below the new tree are some of Dad's ashes. After learning all about Dad from our family, they decided to welcome him back to forever be a part of that special place I was lucky enough to call home.

RUMBLINGS

Trying to understand what makes my never-ending addiction to Tahiti so powerful and all-consuming is why I am taking time to think about my life, analyze it, and write things down. I have asked myself that question over and over, and I have never come up with a satisfactory answer. People who know me say that I must have been a Tahitian in a former life. We laugh at that notion and shake our heads.

Thousands of people take trips every day. They visit places that are beautiful, interesting, magnificent, and inspiring. They come home, resume their lives, and, after a while, plan their next adventure to the next destination on their bucket list. Some people fall in love with just one place. I am one of those people, and Tahiti is one of those places. I've met many other "Tahiti Nuts;" however, I have only met one other person who shares my highly abnormal passion for the place: Jillyn. Meeting her was like getting hit by a lightning bolt. At first, it was shocking to find another one of me, and then it was a bit comforting to know that there was someone else out there who had led a life eerily similar to mine, where just about everybody and everything takes a backseat to the ever-present lure of Tahiti.

When I told a friend I was embarking on a memoir about my love affair with Tahiti, she was silent for a moment, then said, "You are brave. I don't think that I could do anything like that." This friend is brilliant, talented, articulate, and very successful. Her comment surprised me. I said, "Oh, I'm sure you could. All you need to do is to write about something you are passionate about." After a brief hesitation, she replied, "I really don't have anything in my life that I am passionate about." Oh, I thought to myself, I didn't know that people could exist without being passionate about something. A bit embarrassed and feeling like a clueless blond braggart, I changed the subject and asked about the new home she was building. Safer territory.

At the core of my story is the fact that my parents packed up, took off, and left their four kids, home, jobs, responsibilities, and a perfectly nice suburban life to land on an island on the other side of the equator. Without them taking this leap, my own journey may have never taken off. Their leap became my initial stepping stone. Most parents go to Vegas, Lake Tahoe, or even Hawaii for a week. For God's sake, mine went off the deep end.

As a child, I really didn't know my parents. Sure, they were Mom and Dad, but I didn't know what made them tick, what they were excited and passionate about, what made them happy, sad, lonely, or what they longed for. Only hindsight from the vantage point of being an adult has given me a better understanding of their motivations. There were rumblings, however, that even a girl of twelve could hear as the years and months led up to their eventual departure in May of 1961.

First and foremost, Dad led an adventurous and imaginative childhood. He was born and raised on the edge of the ocean. He could step off of his back porch and right into the water of Narragansett Bay, Rhode Island. He was a true waterman. He could swim, free dive, and sail. He could use a speargun, net, or pole to catch every type of sea life. And he knew all about the tides, currents, waves, and wind. He had a passion for sailing, but he could handle any type of boat. He also knew how to navigate by the stars. His favorite reading materials were sea sagas, such as *Mutiny on the Bounty*, *Captains Courageous*, and *White Shadows in the South Seas*. He'd tell us a story almost every night after dinner, mostly about his childhood adventures in and around the ocean. His shenanigans would scare the crap out of today's parents. Many times, in his after-dinner talks, he spoke of "the South Seas" with hushed reverence and filled our minds with images of a faraway, magical place. We also knew about the tropics because we all gathered around the TV and religiously watched *Adventures in Paradise* with him every week.

As a naval officer, he arrived in Hawaii just after the Pearl Harbor bombing. It was pitch black that morning as he stood on the deck of the naval transport. He told me later, and many times over the years, that he could smell the fragrance of the island well before it ever came into sight. It was wartime. He was there for a reason. It was serious business, for sure; however, he fell in love with Hawaii and her people. Despite the war, he remembered those times as some of the best of his life. He and a few fellow officers rented a classic Hawaiian home on Black Point, just past Diamond Head. Their swimming pool, set in a glistening black lava cliff, was filled by the salt water of breaking waves. The guys had a rollicking good time in that house, and they even adopted a house mascot, a pet monkey. Dad bought an old 1934 Ford that motored him all over the island. Hawaii was made for men like him.

Mom, straight from Southern California, was in Hawaii, too. She came over to help assemble aircraft at Hickam Field. Mom could swim well enough; however, she rarely put her head underwater in an attempt to preserve her hairdo. Due to that fact alone, she could never be classified as a waterwoman. Raised in a more affluent family, her reins were not as loose as Dad's, and her experiences were not as broad. Mom was most interested in meeting people. She was exceptionally friendly and articulate. She was also quite a beauty.

We never knew too much about their meeting, courtship, or falling in love. Finding out about your parents' love affair is entering taboo territory. I do know that they met at a party one night. Mom's picture had been in the Honolulu newspaper the day before. It showed her in the cockpit of a fighter plane welding parts onto the control panel. As the story goes, Dad saw her picture and told his buddies that he'd like to meet *her*. I also know from personal experience that there is something about the tropics that magically modifies just about every emotion. Love, in the embrace of a tropical island, enhanced by the uncertainties of wartime, led me to assume that their love affair was intense and all-consuming.

Having the romantic history of their union set in Hawaii certainly must have added to their desire to someday return to Polynesia. Possibly after years of marriage, family obligations, and the daily suburban grind, the memory of their time in Hawaii may have encouraged them to take that leap to Tahiti to see if that magic could be rekindled.

Another "rumble" was the slow and steady stream of books and magazines about the South Pacific that began to appear on our bookshelf in the living room on Valencia Mesa Drive. Most were nonfiction, written by men, and chronicled a sailing adventure recently made through Polynesia. They were filled with enchanting photographs of places, people, and all things Polynesian. The book collection kept steadily growing. Dad read every word with great interest, studied the maps and charts, memorized every photograph, and took careful notes directly on the books' pages.

There was one last "rumble factor" that most likely played a key part in the planning of my parents' eventual escape to the other side of the equator: soon an airport would be complete in Pape'ete, ready to welcome flights from all over the world. This was huge news. I recall Dad making a dinnertime announcement to that effect one night, and he could barely contain himself. Previously, visitors to Tahiti arrived aboard the *SS Mariposa* or the *SS Monterey*. These cruise ships followed the long-established sea route between San Francisco and Australia via Pape'ete. Passengers could spend a few frantic days on the island before continuing on to their final destination. Dad's dream was to stay in Tahiti, hunker down in a hut on the beach, have an outrigger canoe and some fishing gear, get to know the people and the island, and live the Tahitian way.

Looking back, I don't remember my parents saying much out loud about their upcoming trip, but now I can see in retrospect that there were little indicators everywhere. Most likely, Mom and Dad did not want to scare us kids out of our wits. Kids like to have their parents at home. When they are not home, everything goes kablooey. I can't imagine the excitement they must have felt and how hard it was to not be able to express that enthusiasm by yelling at the top of their lungs, "We are off to Tahiti. Goodbye to everyone we know and everything normal and sane. See you all in a few months."

— POSTSCRIPT —

I am fortunate enough to be the current caretaker of my dad's Polynesian book collection. Over the years, I have read them all. Some of my favorites I have read repeatedly, never tiring of their stories. Coming upon his random handwritten notes as I turn a page always takes my breath away.

THE TRIP

Life rolled along at Valencia Mesa Drive, with triumphs, tragedies, and the normal amount of family drama. Despite any ups and downs, we were a fairly well-adjusted family. Highlights of my childhood included horseback trips in the Sierra Nevada backcountry; beach time on Balboa Island in Newport Beach, California; sailing Newport Bay in little Lido 14s; and family art nights. Near the top of my "Favorite Family Memory" list was the miniature paddle wheel boat Dad made for us. It had little black smokestacks, stenciled on windows painted red, and working paddle wheels attached to a hand crank and a rudder assembly. It could hold three kids. We'd crank the paddle wheels, set the tiller, and paddle off. We'd explore all over Newport Bay, especially the little fingers and inlets around Balboa Island. Nobody knew what to make of that little boat. It was one of a kind and cute as hell. People hooted and hollered at us everywhere we went. Along with our paddle wheel boat, Dad made two beautiful wooden paddleboards. He also made a dolly. We called it the "Fairy Godmother." It was triangular, had wheels at each corner, and could pivot and roll with ease. Our Fairy Godmother helped us get the boards and boat down to the beach on our own when we stayed each summer on Balboa Island. Dad's homemade creations gave us endless hours of fun and, at the same time, built our confidence in and around the ocean.

Two additions joined the family about the same time: a little brother, Kip, and a pool. I was ten by then, and having a baby in the house and a pool in the backyard was thrilling to me. For some reason, I remember the exact dimensions of the pool: eighteen feet by forty-five feet. Leave it to the artist/engineer in Dad to come up with such pleasing dimensions.

To fit the new pool, we had to get rid of more of the lovely orange trees. In their place, we planted tropical plants and palms, and we installed a bamboo fence. Dad also designed and built a change booth of our very own. It was not as elaborate as the one at the Barkers', but nevertheless, we had one. Dad and Mom hoped that all the kids would use it for wet bathing suits and towels; however, we were never properly trained. Slowly, the little change booth became the storage place for miscellaneous family toys, among which was my very first surfboard, an emerald green affair of more than nine feet—single fin.

One morning when I was in sixth grade, Mom drove us to school. Mom's "limousine service" normally only happened on rainy days. Usually, we walked up and down the long hill on Euclid Avenue and delivered ourselves to school and back each day. That morning, Mom pulled up to the curb in her 1956 Chevy two-tone wagon, put the car in park, got out, and gave us each a hug. She left us there on the sidewalk. As she drove away, I looked at the back of her blond poof of hair in the driver's seat and wondered if I'd ever see her again. Tears stung my eyes, and then I turned and walked into class. Sure, our parents had left us over the years for getaways to Las Vegas or Palm Springs, but I could feel that this was something completely different.

I don't recall much hubbub before that departure day in May of 1961. I remember seeing my dad fiddling with a speargun and diving mask. I remember him showing me a pair of tan shoes with very thick rubber soles. He said he'd need to wear them swimming because of poisonous fish that camouflage themselves to look like harmless rocks. Step on one of those, and it was over. Mom, always very fashionable, most likely picked out some perfectly coordinated tops and shorts and some razzle-dazzle dresses for her suitcase.

The one thing I did know was that the Sevilles were going to stay with us for the whole time Mom and Dad were gone. They were a kindly older couple, very old-school. Mrs. Seville had a long gray, greasy braid that she wrapped 'round and 'round her head and attached to her skull with old-fashioned combs. At night, she would let the entire mane loose, and the tips of her hair would fall well below her waist. Mr. Seville was the custodian at our school. He had very large teeth that were crooked and yellowing. He wore old jean bib overalls and chunky work boots. Mrs. Seville was one of our regular babysitters. Mr. Seville only showed up if Mom and Dad were out of town for a weekend. I guess on those overnight babysitting assignments, two adults were needed to contain the tribe.

Things were very different with the Sevilles at the helm for the four Roberts kids. They placed a plate with neatly stacked sliced white bread every night on the table for dinner as a "side dish." Mr. Seville gobbled them up as if there was no tomorrow. Mrs. Seville served mysterious food that was always drenched in a thick, brown gravy, which she served with a side of overcooked vegetables. It was a far cry from what we were used to: barbecued burgers, tacos, Mom's lasagna, and maybe spaghetti every now and then for a change of pace.

Besides the food, we were all traumatized by the introduction of religion into our daily lives. Sure, we went to the First Presbyterian Church up the road on Christmas Eve, but that was about it in the religion department during our upbringing. The Sevilles were *very* religious, and not just in a Methodist, Catholic, or Baptist way. They were Holy Rollers. That meant we were to go with them to their church every Wednesday evening and all day on Sunday. In their church, a simple little frame house, people cried in the aisles while holding soggy tissues to their faces. They fell to the floor, screaming about seeing the Lord. They walked up the aisle like zombies with raised hands to receive salvation on the stage. They played loud church music with electric guitars, an instrument that I had previously believed was reserved for rock bands. It was scary for all four of us, and it made for agonizingly long Sundays.

My other memory of that time was of the stern and serious words that Dad repeated monotonously before they left: "Watch Kip in the pool every second." Kip was still very young, and the pool was very new. If my parents had any reservations at all about leaving the gang behind and setting off for Tahiti, it was the fear of Kip falling in the pool and drowning. In every letter they sent home, Dad wrote those exact words. He used capital letters and underlined that mantra: <u>WATCH KIP IN THE POOL EVERY SECOND</u>! I'm positive that the Sevilles did not know how to swim. That left Kip's life in our small hands. As instructed, we watched him every second that he was in the pool.

Postcards, featherweight airmail letters, and small packages arrived in our mailbox at regular intervals from Mom and Dad. In some of the small packages were slides and reels of 8 mm movies. In those days, film had to be shipped directly from your vacation spot to Connecticut for development. From there, the reels were shipped to your home. Many of these reels made it back home before Mom and Dad. Brice, being about fifteen at the time, had some understanding of how to set up and run Dad's rickety, clacky old projector. Through the miracle of film and technology, we got to preview some of their adventures even before they set foot back through our kitchen door. Of particular interest to Brice were the images of topless Tahitian beauties. His fifteen-year-old self couldn't help but stop the film on their luscious nakedness, so much so that he nearly burned holes in those frames of film—a testament to teenage male hormones.

It was also during this time that Brice decided to uproot all of Mom's prized rosebushes out in the front yard. She had propagated and cared for the two circular flower beds next to our cement driveway with the utmost dedication. Year after year, she painstakingly pulled weeds, fertilized, and pruned her prized roses. Each spring, her efforts rewarded us all with exotic, fragrant blooms. Nobody, including Brice, knew exactly why he pulled out all her roses. It's one of those mysteries that will forever remain unsolved. I do know that after that murderous affair, Mom never planted another rose bush. She stuck with daisies.

Somehow, some way, we four got along without our parents for several months. I counted the days until their expected return. What came through the door on the appointed day and hour was something completely unexpected. Mom and Dad had left us as two overworked and deflated suburban parents: Dad was exhausted from his intense job at North American Aviation and Mom was physically and mentally drained from her duties as mother to four kids and a household full of endless responsibilities. Two people I barely recognized burst through the front door that day: A bronzed, muscled god of a man and a similarly glowing goddess of a woman with hair so blond it shocked me. Both were dressed in bright island clothing, and each had strands and strands of shell leis around their neck. They each sported a woven *pandanus* hat just like the ones I had seen at the Barkers'. Smiles were white and broad, and eyes were sparkling and happier than I had ever seen before. Not only did they look as vibrant as teenagers, but they simply *were* different in every way imaginable. Things were about to change in the Roberts household. And change, in a delightful way, they did.

— *POSTSCRIPT* —

Dad's paddle wheel boat became a sensation. Some boatbuilders "bought" the idea, although Dad never saw a penny. The little paddle wheeler was mass produced in fiberglass for Newport Dunes, a back bay playground for Orange County families in the early 1960s. I never knew what became of the original one made of plywood or our rolling, triangular Fairy Godmother. I kept the two sleek, wooden paddleboards in my garage in Dana Point, California, for many years. When rainwater leaked on them, concerned for their safety, I gave them to a surf pal with a dry garage. He eventually disappeared into the desert. Although I tried, the paddleboards were never to be seen again—one of my deepest regrets. Dad's camera, projector, and reels are at Brice's house in the Bay Area. Mom's travel journal and all of their incredible slides are right here in my office in Kona.

MEANWHILE . . . ON THE OTHER SIDE OF THE EQUATOR

On my birthday several years ago, Dad handed me a small gift. We were all out on our lanai in Kona, having dinner by candlelight. I opened the wrapping and immediately recognized the little book. It was Mom's Tahiti travel journal. I began to read aloud right then and there. The dim light and her strange, backward-slanted handwriting made me falter. Nevertheless, I was thrilled to have it. After blowing out the candles on a fluffy *haupia* cake, I vowed to all in attendance that I would not only read it, but I would transcribe Mom's words onto my computer. My plan was to type one day's journal entry each afternoon of my summer vacation. That seemed like an attainable goal. Little did I know that transcribing Mom's Tahiti journal would be the highlight of my day all summer long.

As I began to type that first day, I discovered that I could not stop at just one day's entry. I already knew many of their stories; however, the details of their daily comings and goings intrigued me. On and on I typed. I felt like a little angelic Peeping Tom, sitting on Mom's shoulder. I had a front-row seat to all of their Tahitian travels. By that time, Mom had been gone for almost twenty years. As I read her words and typed away, she sprang back, larger than life.

I called Dad after a few days into the project. I had an idea: I'd email him what I typed, and he would type his two cents worth as a postscript to each of Mom's daily entries. So that's just what we did. When it was complete, I compiled all the pages into little booklets. I centered a classic photo of Mom and Dad paddling a canoe in Tahitian waters on the cover. It was my Christmas gift to Brice, Stephanie, and Kip the following December.

I opened my copy of the little book I created and reread it this morning. Now that Dad's also gone, his words mean more to me than ever before. Mom and Dad wrote from totally different perspectives. Mom focused on the wild cast of interesting characters, the parties, the tropical homes, and the exotic food and drink. Dad concentrated on the pure magic of Tahiti's natural world and all they discovered in the lagoons, on the beaches, and in the valleys and streams. He also fell in love with the Tahitian people, their friendliness, simple way of living, overflowing love, and acceptance. He was completely captivated by Polynesian facial features. He made many thumbnail sketches of Polynesian faces that he would later transpose into oil paint or charcoal renderings.

It all began when Mom and Dad took off on the very first flight from Los Angeles into the newly created landing strip at Fa'a'a. There's a great photo of Mom at LAX standing on the tarmac next to their plane. She was dressed in a tweed suit, wore high heels, and held a matching handbag. Her blond hair is perfectly coiffed. She's proudly holding up an amenity from the now-gone TAI Airlines: a bottle of French champagne. Their flight took off from Los Angeles and headed southwest. Dad was forty, and Mom was thirty-six.

Weeks before leaving, they used a radiophone to call Tahiti. They somehow radioed a *vahine* named Pepe. "*Oui!*" Pepe said over the crackling line, "I have a house for rent." They rented Pepe's house sight unseen, and all was set. Today, we would all use Google Earth to zoom in on the location and see the house, the yard, and the neighborhood. In 1961, you just took your chances. After a few restless nights on a less than desirable and very noisy downtown Papeete street, they decided to find another place. Thankfully, by then Mom and Dad had met their Tahitian savior, a friendly *vahine* from the Australs. Her name was Big Louise. She knew of a house for rent right on the sand in Puna'auia. The house was just what they wanted. Thatched in the traditional style, it had running water, rudimentary indoor plumbing, some basic electricity (twenty-watt bulbs only), and an outrigger canoe. This became their home base for the remainder of their days in Tahiti. It was perfect.

Mom and Dad hunkered down and began to live the Tahitian way. They learned how to get around the maze of buzzing streets in Pape'ete and all along the curvy and winding Broom Road that circled the island. They started out with a scooter and then later rented a funny little European car. It regularly broke down and had flat tires. Every time it broke down, they would curse that pint-size car. A few hours later, they would bless that little car. Its repair seemed to always lead them on a brand-new adventure where they would meet a brand-new cast of characters who helped them get the car back up and running. They got to know their neighbors, the stretch of beach out front, and—most importantly—the lagoon that teemed with fish. Directly in front of their thatched house across the Sea of the Moon was the island of Mo'orea. Having that enchanting outline as their backdrop for every sunrise and sunset was "breathtaking," as Mom wrote.

They met a cast of real characters. Most of their new friends were Tahitians and local immigrants from China and France. Americans were still somewhat of a rarity at that time; however, there was a small number of American expats already getting established in Tahiti. Some were starting businesses, some were developing plantations, and others were simply very wealthy and were there for the sheer indulgence of being able to live on such a beautiful island. It was an incredible and dynamic mix of people. Everyone welcomed my parents with open arms that stretched very, very wide. Mom and Dad were invited to every gathering, of which there were many. They met and made many lifelong friends, many of whom I would meet over the ensuing years.

My parents spent hours every day in the lagoon in their outrigger. They would paddle together and find a diving spot among the coral heads. Mom would hold down the fort in the anchored canoe while Dad dove the wrecks, explored the coral heads, and used his speargun to bring home a fresh catch for the dinner table. He would string the fish on a line tied to his waist. One day a shark began to circle him with his string of bleeding fish. From behind a large coral head, Dad kept his spear trained on the shark's black and heartless eyes as Mom struggled to pull the anchor and solo paddle to pick him up. After that, he saw sharks and barracuda every time he dove. From then on, he was more careful with how he hauled his catch along behind him.

Adding to the already potent mix of personalities were the cast and crew of the MGM production, *Mutiny on the Bounty*. They had been filming in Tahiti for several months. Hundreds of locals were on the set. Hollywood stars and extras were there, too. Naturally, in such a small place, Mom and Dad met everyone. Dad was invited to be an extra in the movie. The costume designer dressed him in pantaloons and a swarthy shirt, added a wig with a ponytail, and topped it all off with a cloth sailor's cap. God, he was handsome. He made exactly fifty francs a day, or five US dollars.

During their first days in Tahiti, they met one of the

famous Bali Hai Boys, Hugh Kelly, and his *vahine*, Dallas. Kelly invited Mom and Dad over to his place on Mo'orea for a party. Dad stocked up on demijohns of wine and cases of beer, and then off they went across the Sea of the Moon on the small ferry, the *Moana Tide*. One of the earliest hotels in French Polynesia, the Bali Hai Hotel, was in its earliest form and still a bit rough. As it turns out, the "party" was a traditional Tahitian *tama'ara'a*. Planning, preparation, and feasting went on for five glorious days. In addition to eating, drinking, singing, and dancing, there were explorations by canoe, hikes up rivers, shrimp-hunting expeditions, and icy swims in freshwater pools. The people of Mo'orea welcomed Mom and Dad with open arms. During their stay, Dad repaired one of Kelly's small outboard engines. Kelly must have thought that Dad was an OK guy because he asked him right then and there if he'd like to become a partner in the Bali Hai Hotel. While I'm sure Dad gave that some very serious thought, it never came to pass, and I continued growing up among the orange trees of Sunny Hills instead of the coconut palms of Mo'orea.

After returning to Puna'auia and their thatched home, Mom and Dad decided to try to make a trip to Bora Bora. It took several trips to Pape'ete to make the arrangements. There were several false starts, the result of the flight getting repeatedly canceled. Finally, the stars aligned, and off they went in an immense seaplane, a Sunderland 500. Mom wrote of the "thrilling" water takeoffs and landings. Spray flew up to cover the passenger's windows. The Sunderland made a short stop in Raiatea. They took the launch ashore and had just enough time for a walk down the main drag of Uturoa. A photo of Mom shows her standing in the village street. She's wearing her custom dress made at Marie Ah You in Pape'ete. In the shadows is an immense pig tied to a tree, and in the background are the fronts of a few small shops.

What they saw as they approached Bora Bora in the Sunderland took their breath away. Dad's photos from the seaplane that day are magnificent and an exquisite documentation of "how it used to be." In 1961, the island was totally natural and undeveloped. There were only a few thatched houses, one small village, and a scattering of boats. The surrounding *motu* (small islets on the fringing reef) were bare of anything except a few copra (dried coconut) sheds. The road was sand. The only development of any significance was the recently created Hotel Bora Bora on Matira Beach (what was considered at the time to be the queen of Tahitian hotels and is no longer in existence). Mom and Dad spent one night in a shoddy *pension* (modest guest house) in the main village of Vaitape and, after a wild ride with a three-to-a-motor scooter, moved over to the Hotel Bora Bora.

The hotel was heaven on earth, a dream-come-true sort of place. It was in its first days of operation, and staff were still working the kinks out, but nobody cared. It turned out there was no bartender yet. There were some thirsty guests, so Dad, who was a decent mixologist, jumped over the top of the smooth wood bar and became the bartender, mixing up all manner of liquid refreshment. I can just see him moving that cocktail shaker to the beat of the ever-present Tahitian drums playing on and on in the hotel bar. The nightly rate at Hotel Bora Bora was fifty US dollars, quite an extravagant price at that time. While there, they were treated to a lagoon tour in a sleek wooden skiff. Alex Bourgerie, the hotel's first manager, was at the helm. His *vahine*, the incredibly famous Paumotu singer, Marie Mariterangi, was by his side. Mom and Dad were in the second open-air cockpit. There was a *mara'amu* blowing in from the southeast. Though this cold, windy storm put a slight damper on things, my parents never, ever stopped raving about Bora Bora.

Their days in Tahiti were coming to an end. They were going to continue to Fiji and explore the Yasawa Islands. In the days before they left Tahiti, all their new friends, who felt like dear old friends, stopped into the modest house in Puna'auia to say goodbye. Big Louise even began to cry at the thought of "losing them."

— *POSTSCRIPT* —

Big Louise and her husband, Bruce, ended up in Hanalei on Kauai. They opened the Tahiti Nui Bar. Mom, Dad, Big Louise, and Bruce remained friends for life. When on Kauai, Dad was always put to work helping her serve the buffet dinners at the Nui. One day, a few years ago, I stopped in to say 'iaorana *(a greeting) to Big Louise. She didn't recognize me, but when I told her who my parents were, she grabbed my arm and held it tight. She cried right then and there and told me that I looked just like my mom. I cried, too.*

Last Mother's Day, I posted that photo of my mom standing in the street in Uturoa on my Facebook page. I love Mom's spirit in that picture. A longtime and very dear friend, Hina, saw it. She said that her heart skipped a beat to suddenly see that picture up on her computer screen. It turns out her parent's store, which also served as Hina's childhood home, was clearly visible in the background of that photo. We couldn't help but wonder if our parents had met.

Dad made one of his ships in a bottle while in Tahiti. He learned the craft as a child and was famous for making them. This one was the HMS Bounty. *He took all his modeling tools down with him and worked on the project whenever he had a little spare time. Just before they left for Fiji, he gave that boat in a bottle to Pepe. It was a "thank you" to her for letting them move to another house and kindly returning their rent money.*

AFTERGLOW

The Sevilles packed their clothes after their long babysitting stint at our house and went home, both barely intact. Mission accomplished: all the Roberts kids survived. No more Holy Roller indoctrinations on Sunday. Thankfully, we could revert to being glorious heathens once again. Mom and Dad's tans soon faded. They hung their vibrant clothing up at the back of their closet and put away all the shell leis. Dad's speargun and dive mask returned to the change booth out by the pool with all the other family water toys. I never saw his swimming shoes with thick rubber soles return from the South Seas. Mom got back to her usual motherly duties, and Dad resumed his trek to the corporate world in a suit and tie. Everything returned to normal. Well . . . not quite. Some things had changed on Valencia Mesa.

Dad loved to view his Tahitian photography endlessly. That meant the clackity old movie projector and its companion, the unruly slide projector, got set up on Saturday nights. “Who wants to see the Tahiti pictures?” he'd yell out. At first, we all ran at top speed to the sunken family room. We fought over the best seats in the house. The screen would already be set up in front of the fireplace, and off we would go to the South Pacific again. It was like watching *Adventures in Paradise*, except Mom and Dad were the stars in place of Gardner McKay. After a while, one by one, family members started to disappear from the viewing audience, eventually even Mom. For some reason, however, I never tired of his spectacular photos. I was front row and center at every showing. The look on his face as reflected in the light of the projected images was worth the price of admission for me. As he looked at each image, his commentary reflected his complete and utter awe of the subject matter. It was obvious: he was in love with Tahiti.

Along with the slide and movie shows came the introduction of Tahitian music. Suddenly, our sleek 1950s hi-fi cabinet no longer played Frank Sinatra LPs. In place of Frank's smooth-as-silk vocals came the overpowering pounding of Tahitian drums, the flat-toned singing of the *vahines*, and the high-pitched twang of Tahitian *utureres* (ukuleles). Never mind that the music was in a language that made no sense to me. I can't imagine where my parents obtained those LPs in Orange County during the 1960s. Just like their book collection, their record collection kept steadily growing. All day on Saturday and Sunday those powerfully rhythmic records would beat, beat, beat out through the entire house and all over the backyard. The furious drumming had all four kids moving like hip-swinging banshees as we completed our weekend chores in record time. Slowly, little by little, I began to sing along to the alluring songs. They were in a language I did not know, but for some mystical reason, I just couldn't help myself.

There was also a "shrine" of sorts in the sunken family room. A beautiful *tanoa* bowl carved out of smooth, dark Polynesian wood was nestled in a corner bookcase. It was carefully packed and carried home from the South Seas. Mom and Dad filled the bowl with all of the shells they found. The shells were otherworldly. Somehow, I kept finding myself at that bowl. Looking. Feeling. Admiring. Wondering. I held the shells in my hands and marveled at the tangible objects that took me far away to a place that was building inside my mind, a place to be desired, a place to love, and a place I began to long for.

One evening, not long after their return, the entire family piled into the Chevy wagon and made the drive to Hollywood. *Mutiny on the Bounty* was in its exclusive engagement at Grauman's Chinese Theatre. Mom and Dad wanted to see the movie after meeting all the actors and being on the set. Dad was hoping that he would make the final cut. We never saw Dad, and we decided that he must have ended up on the proverbial cutting room floor. For some reason, he didn't care. Being a small part of one of his favorite childhood sea sagas was good enough for him.

The final afterglow of that trip was the most important one for me. The *tama'ara'a*s soon became a regular part of our lives. Mom's kitchen revved into high gear with all sorts of unusual activity. Dad's long cocktail bar hummed with whirling blenders and the jingle jangle of clinking glasses. The backyard, already rather tropical, got magically transformed into a jungle scene. All the while, those drums throbbed from the hi-fi speakers as the swirling party preparations went on. Dad even made a "gut bucket." He had discovered this musical instrument in Tahiti. It is the South Seas version of a stand-up bass. Making one involved melding together an old, galvanized wash tub, a length of rope, and a mop handle. He could play the gut bucket well, but then again, anybody could. That was the beauty of this homemade instrument. The exotic guests attending these *tama'ara'as* were Mom and Dad's co-conspirators in South Pacific adventures. They arrived from all over Southern California and Tahiti. The partying would go on well into the night. The *vahines* would dance the hip-shaking, traditional dance of Tahiti, the *tamure*, and the *tanes* would gather together in an impromptu band. During these parties, I was supposed to already be asleep in bed. Of course, sleep was always the farthest thing from my mind. I would sit on the stairs in the gray shadows and watch the partiers in all their joyful abandon. I believe that was when I swallowed the lure, the lure of Tahiti.

— *POSTSCRIPT* —

It was at the first of the tama'ara'as *that I met real Tahitians. I have forgotten who they were, except for Big Louise. There was just something about her. Ask anyone in Hanalei.*

To this day I still do a lot of my cleaning to my Pandora channel titled "Tahitian." The beat, as always, has me moving double time. There are some songs I hear that instantly whisk me back to Valencia Mesa and that old hi-fi system. The old classics are still being played. I can still sing along. The only difference is that now I know what the lyrics mean.

Right here on my desk is a framed movie poster from Mutiny on the Bounty. *It's a beautiful rendering of some of the scenes, including images of Marlon Brando and the sensuous Tahitian female lead, Tarita Teri'ipaia. Dad's photo is inserted in the collage. He's in his MGM sailor's getup. It's my favorite picture of him.*

Part Two

All those years ago, as a small child sitting on that stairway in the dark, I swallowed the lure. I've never figured out why none of my siblings took the bait.

As soon as I was a bona fide adult, I began to take frequent trips to Tahiti. Once I began, I could not stop, nor did I want to. In those early days, I began to learn to live the Tahitian way. I started speaking Tahitian and experienced exotic love with a rascal of a *tane*. I had many wild adventures and made lifelong friends in my beautiful, alluring Tahiti. I have written several stories about those early days; however, where I ended up as a seventy-something woman with my husband by my side is the real story.

My Kona friends kept asking me, "What do you do down there? How can you leave Hawaii? What's an atoll? Are you bored? Are there other people there? Are there any stores? What do you eat? What's your house like?" I tried to explain it all, but I could never quite paint a complete and accurate picture. One day, fresh from a swim, the light bulb went on. I finally knew what to do. With a towel wrapped around my waist and sand in between my toes, I set up my iPad and I began to write. My stories, all written here on the atoll, will hopefully answer these questions and more.

FINDING MY ATOLL

Sitting in my big, blue chair under the broad, shiny leaves of the *tou* tree by the edge of this magnificent lagoon, I'm thinking back. I'm thinking way, way back. This is the story of how the whole thing began: my long-term love affair with Rangiroa, one of the most spectacular corners in all of French Polynesia.

It was 1985. Laura sat across from me at her tidy desk. She was attractive, young, efficient, and accomplished. I say accomplished because at a relatively young age, she and her business partner, Leah, had successfully built a boutique travel agency. South Pacific Travel was located on a quiet side street in the old Cannery district of Newport Beach.

I was at Laura's desk planning a three-month South Pacific adventure. The previous summer I had a spur-of-the-moment trip to Tahiti. As I've written, I have been in love with Tahiti since I was a very young girl, ever since my parents "infected" me with the "Tahiti Disease" that they had caught during their extended stay in French Polynesia in 1961. My first trip six months prior was to Mo'orea and Bora Bora. Those two weeks were enough to reel me in hook, line, and sinker. I wanted more Tahiti, and Laura was helping me.

As we were plotting my itinerary, Laura suddenly said, "You need to go to Rangiroa." I'd never heard that word before, and I countered with, "What's Rangiroa?" Her simple reply was, "It's an atoll, the second largest atoll in the world. You need to see it." She continued, "They say of Rangi . . . only sand, sea, and sky." Sand, sea, and sky, I thought. Sign me up. I wondered what an atoll was, but I really didn't care. All I knew for sure was that I wanted to go.

In the mid-1980s, Rangiroa was exactly as advertised—sand, sea, and sky. There was very little else. My sister, Stephanie, joined me on that leg of my adventure. We stayed at the Kia Ora Hotel (what is now the Kia Ora Resort and Spa). The word "hotel" may have been a misnomer. At that time, the Kia Ora consisted of a few simple bungalows scattered along a narrow strand of brilliant, white sand. A small, thatched open-air stand in a central locale served as the reception desk. There was a restaurant of sorts serving modest meals. It was beautifully decorated with hanging shell light fixtures high above the dining tables. A smooth wood railing encircling the restaurant was constructed of burnished branches from the *tou* tree. I remember being surprised to see anatomically correct penises carved in the branches as part of the decor. The Kia Ora Hotel was the creation of three Frenchmen. To even think that they could build a functioning hotel in the remote and wild Tuamotus at that time was, in my mind at least, nothing short of visionary.

The big attraction was, and remains to this day, the atoll itself. Rangiroa is an almost unfathomable marvel, created by nature and time. To get a feel for the atoll, Stephanie and I took an all-day boat trip south to Les Sables Roses with a blond, local kid named Toriki. His *vahine* and their shaggy dog rounded out the crew. Getting to Pink Sands took a little more than an hour. As we sped along in Toriki's boat, I was mesmerized by the endless combinations of sand, sea, and sky: islands of every configuration and size; twisting beaches; pocket coves; long, white empty beaches; inlets of turquoise blue; huge white cotton candy clouds standing tall in the open sky; and the translucent lagoon itself. If I looked carefully, I could also see the open ocean and waves breaking with fury on the outside of the atoll. Of course, added to the mix were millions upon millions of coconut palms waving their *'iaorana* as we passed. There were a few thatched huts and a smattering of tin boats tied off to tree trunks. Aside from that, I could spot nothing more.

Once at Pink Sands, Toriki got busy catching lagoon fish; he then built a fire using dried branches and coconut husks. As he barbequed the fresh fish, his *vahine* expertly set up an impromptu dining table in the sand under the shade of the palms. She then walked around picking broad, shiny leaves that were to be our dining plates. As they prepared our picnic, Stephanie and I explored Pink Sands. We marveled at the overwhelming, wide-open beauty. We both lounged lazily at the edge of the lagoon. The warm water enveloped us; it was like being embraced by soft velvet. Over and over, I rolled in the pristine pink sand in a state of complete and utter joy. The lapping water rinsed me off after each glorious wave. It was that day, I believe, I found my personal paradise.

Our stay in Rangiroa was short, a mere three days. Each day was enchanting. No matter what we did, my eyes seemed to be constantly riveted to the view of the endless turquoise of the lagoon. I couldn't get enough of that magical color. At the end of our stay, we sadly packed our bags, paid our bill, and climbed on board Le Truck (an open-air bus). As we made our way back to the pocket-size airport, I vividly remember thinking that I wasn't ready to leave. Something about this place struck a chord deep within me. Rangiroa and I were meant for each other. I would return, that much I knew.

That first trip to Rangiroa was almost forty years ago. At the time, I simply could not wrap my head around the alluring beauty of it all. It's hard for me to believe that all these years later, I have built a life here with my husband. The lure of this place has never let go of its hold on me. We travel along that same route to Pink Sands very often in our own boat these days. I still have trouble taking this place in: its immensity; the story of its formation; and its ongoing and ever-present evolution of sand, sea, and sky as dictated by the tides, waves, and wind.

— POSTSCRIPT —

About a year ago, I thought of Laura. Naturally, I googled her. I wanted to tell her where I had ended up and to offer my thanks to her for helping me find my atoll. Like me, she had moved to Hawaii. She raised two sons on Oahu and led a full life. Sadly, she committed suicide before I could reconnect with her. I'm regretful that I didn't try to find her sooner.

Toriki is still in Rangiroa. He no longer runs excursions. He has built some beautiful bungalows on his property and is enjoying being the host to people from all over the world who come to see the atoll. He and his family have become our friends. One night, as a group of us sat on our lanai enjoying a lasagna dinner, I pulled up some old photos of that first trip to Les Sables Roses way back in 1985. Toriki and I were shocked to discover that he was the guy who took me on my first adventure in Rangiroa. We simply became friends through happenstance over the past few years. He and I had never made that connection before. He recognized his boat and his furry little dog. We had a pretty good laugh over that coincidence.

FORMATION OF AN ATOLL

From our lanai, I can see straight out to a myriad of shimmering blues. Turquoise shallows turn to darker blues and then finally to the cobalt blue of the long, curving horizon. Yes, you heard that right: this lagoon is so immense that it has its own horizon. Beyond the horizon is the other side of the atoll, which cannot be seen from here.

Looking out, I often try to imagine that long ago there was an island in the middle of this lagoon. That's the generally accepted scientific theory of how atolls are formed. A high island with its fringing coral reef is the beginning stage. As time passes, the island erodes into the ocean and finally disappears, leaving only the coral outer ring. Coral is a living entity that continues to slowly grow over time. Thus, the living ring remains even though its partner in creation, the high island, left long ago.

There are seventy-eight coral atolls flung randomly across

these South Pacific waters. Collectively, they are called the Tuamotus. The Tuamotus are just one of the five island groups that make up French Polynesia. They are also called the Low Islands or the Dangerous Islands. Ask any sailor about making the approach to an atoll. They will confirm the "dangerous" part of the name.

The best way to observe an atoll is from the air. From above, you can see the basic elements of its geographic structure: a ring of islets (*motu*) circling a central lagoon. Waterways (*hoas*) flow in between the *motu* from lagoon to ocean on an outgoing tide and from ocean to lagoon on an incoming tide. Larger waterways, called passes (*ava*), also flow between the lagoon and the ocean. The world of an atoll is an organic one in which these geographic elements physically change with the winds, tides, storms, and currents.

Motu vary greatly in size. Some are tiny and just big enough to support a coconut palm. Some are immense and stretch for miles. All are fluid in nature and can appear and disappear or completely change overnight. *Motu* are flat and not very wide. From most places on the atoll, you can see the lagoon and ocean just by turning your head back and forth.

Hoas also vary in size and depth. Some are only ankle-deep, some are knee-deep, and some are too deep to traverse by foot. That's when a boat comes in handy. Some days they are calm. Some days they rage with rushing tidal water. Sometimes the *hoas* merge together, and sometimes they disappear under moving sand.

Passes are wide and deep enough to allow larger vessels to enter the lagoon. Rangiroa has two passes. Some atolls have none, causing cargo ships to off-load goods outside the reef onto smaller boats to take ashore. The tidal pull in the passes is extreme. Sometimes whirlpools form, making for very dangerous swimming and diving. For safety, most water activities are scheduled around what the tides are doing and when.

Rangiroa's lagoon is really like a sea. The only word to describe it is, to be redundant, immense. Circumnavigation of the interior of the lagoon by boat could be done comfortably in two or three days, weather permitting. That would include stopping each night at a *motu*. I have heard stories of people who have walked around the atoll. That would have to include some serious swimming in places where the *motu* are sparse. About a year ago, two elite athletes from Pape'ete attempted their own circumnavigation by foot. We followed the story closely. They only made it so far, then had to call it quits. Supposedly, some people have paddled kayaks all the way around, but of that I'm not sure.

One unique geographic feature in Rangiroa is an area called Lagon Bleu. Believe it or not, this is a smaller atoll forming within the main atoll structure. By smaller, I mean its size is comparable to several square city blocks. It has its own ecosystem, *motu,* and *hoas*. Lagon Bleu is the most popular site for visitors. Its extreme beauty is overwhelming, even if you have seen it many times.

Living in such physical fluidity has made us sharpen our

awareness skills. A puff of wind, a current reversal, or a wave out of nowhere are things we watch for carefully and constantly. We act accordingly if there is imminent danger to us, our little shack in the sand, or our boat. We've had one disaster. That's enough.

— *POSTSCRIPT* —

The flora and fauna of an atoll is strikingly different from the other islands of Tahiti. An atoll has no volcanic peaks, no rolling hills, no canopy of lush trees, no meandering rivers, and no rushing waterfalls. Very few land birds call an atoll home, while marine birds and all manner of sea life are in abundance.

Makatea is the only atoll in the Tuamotus that is different. It is a raised atoll. It's circular in shape like its neighboring atolls, but it soars up tall in the South Pacific sky, rising vertically, straight out of the ocean. Makatea has no lagoon, no hoas, *no* motu, *and no beaches. The small village is perched high up on the plateau 260 feet above sea level.*

THE LONG AND WINDING ROAD TO OUR SHACK IN THE SAND

Many people have asked us how we came upon our tiny shack in paradise. When I answer, I usually say something like, "It's a long story" and leave it at that. It truly is a long story, so if you're interested, mix up a cold *maita'i*, put your feet up, and read on. The tale spans more than three decades as we slowly hone in on our favorite place, Rangiroa. Along the way, we fine-tuned our living arrangements, going from simply being hotel guests with all-inclusive meals and activities to 100 percent self-sufficient living. Here's how it happened.

Right off the bat when I first started coming to French Polynesia, I knew that I wanted to live in Tahiti. There was no question in my mind. It was just a matter of figuring out how to do it. I was young and single with few strings attached. It seemed easy enough . . . right? Wrong.

Then, as now, the French require anyone who is not a French citizen to follow strict entry and exit regulations. Non-French citizens are allowed to be in Tahiti for no longer than ninety out of every 180 days. The calculations are a bit complicated if you come in and out of the country as I did for years and as we still do. Bottom line: our time in Tahiti is limited as deemed by French law. We've been asked by several Tahitian friends if they could help us apply for long-term nonresident status. Having that would eliminate the hassle of counting and calculating days in and out of the country. We thought about it and decided just to continue as is: three months in Rangiroa, and three months in Kona on a regular rotation throughout each year, with our goal being 50 percent of each year on the atoll. Staying longer than 50 percent would violate strictly enforced immigration regulations.

I began asking several of the American expats I met early on, "How do you get to stay in Tahiti?" Answers varied; however, they boil down to three things: marry a Tahitian, be able to offer something the French want or need (such as a product, service, or skill), or just be very rich. Well, those options left me out, so I continued coming and going, usually totaling between one and three months per year in French Polynesia.

Thankfully, miraculously, I later met my match, my soulmate, and my eventual husband, Scooter, who jumped right into the program with me. Together we traveled all over Tahiti. We stayed mostly in out-of-the-way places, small hotels, and *pensions*. We met incredibly welcoming people and made many lifelong friends. As time passed, we gravitated toward the Tuamotus because of the overwhelming beauty, wonderful Paumotu people, and wide-open spaces.

On one trip we splurged and booked a stay at Le Sauvage, a magical place on *Motu Ava'e Rahi* (Island of the Full Moon). It was far across the Rangiroa lagoon. We arrived by boat late in the morning on a spectacular atoll day. Five exquisitely crafted *fares* (bungalows) were scattered along the flawless white-sand beach. Unique in design, each *fare* varied slightly in size. All were thatched in the traditional style and all had burnished tree branches as lanai railings and interior support beams. The hanging decorations inside consisted of thousands of shells strung together in every possible artistic configuration. A few pieces of simple, handmade furniture fashioned from local dark hardwoods seamlessly filled the bungalow. There was a sunken bathroom with a loose coral floor. The freshwater shower looked like it was straight off the movie set of *Swiss Family Robinson*. The sink was a giant, white clam shell. There was no electricity, although each *fare* had a kerosene lantern for the total darkness that enveloped the *motu* nights. After Scooter and I dropped our bags in our *fare*, we walked back to the beach, hand in hand. We turned and gazed back at Le Sauvage. We were mesmerized. We had found perfection.

A central dining *fare*, equally as enchanting, was tucked under a stand of tall, feathery *'aito* trees. This was the gathering spot where castaways from every corner of the globe met for candlelit meals, a cold Hinano beer, and some "talk story" (the Polynesian version of conversation). After dinner, communal singing of the old Tahitian songs and traditional dancing commenced. Camaraderie flourished, and language barriers simply disappeared.

As beautiful as Le Sauvage was, there was something even better there: our hosts, Teiva and his *vahine*, Meho. Teiva was charismatic, fun-loving, and full of local knowledge. Meho was beautiful, warm, and welcoming with a wealth of Paumotu know-how. Meho's mother, Tuaore; Tuaore's *tane*, Raimana; and Meho's cousin, Tiare, rounded out the crew. These people were irresistible. Everything about them drew us in. They were fun, funny, knowledgeable, adventuresome, warm, loving, inviting, good-hearted, and kind—the complete package.

We didn't know it at the time, but this small group of people would actually change the course of our journey. There's no other way to put it; we simply fell in love with them. Something just clicked between us. From that point on, Rangiroa became our one and only destination in French Polynesia, and Teiva and Meho became our friends.

Over the next few years, we bounced around from place to place on the atoll, usually staying in family-owned guest houses. Sometimes we splurged and stayed at the Kia Ora Hotel, which had grown into a posh resort and spa by then. We made a few more magical trips to Le Sauvage as well.

One day, when we were guests at the Kia Ora, a lovely *vahine* who worked there approached me. She asked simply, "Why do you stay here in the hotel for a month?" I responded honestly with, "Because we love Rangiroa so much." She replied, "Why don't you rent a house?" A house? I hadn't realized that there were any houses for rent here. She assured me that there were, and, in fact, her boyfriend's cousin had one. Really? We were departing the next day, but we made a few phone calls and arranged to go see the rental house before our flight.

As arranged, a car arrived at the Kia Ora the next morning to pick us up. It was right on time. Inside were two *vahines* that epitomized the warmth of Polynesia: Tarona and her mother, Tumai. They drove a short distance down the road, then turned down a sandy driveway that wove naturally through a palm grove. At the end sat a cluster of three houses. One house was by the road. The next house, in the middle, was surrounded by a lush tropical garden with brilliant blooms on every bush. Then they led us to the house that was up for rent. It was on a sandy beach a few feet from the lagoon. It reminded us of the *fares* at Le Sauvage. We walked around, looking high and low inside the house, genuinely admiring the quality of the construction and the view. We walked out on the beach and cruised through the sandy side yards. We asked a few questions, but our minds were already made up. It was perfect. We loved it. We agreed to rent it for our next stay, the entire month of May. What luck.

That month in our shack in the sand worked out so well. Our hosts took us in like family. We shared an occasional meal, had a few adventures together, and got to know each other. They were lovely people, hardworking, honest, and fun. We could not have been happier. A few days before our stay was up, we saw a big sign out by the road tacked to a coconut tree. It said: *MAISON À LOUER* (house for rent). Uh oh, we thought, this house would get snapped up like nobody's business, and we'll never get back in. And that's exactly what happened. Over the next ten years, I called Tarona on a regular basis to see if, by chance, we could stay in the house again for our next trip. The answer was always the same: "Sorry, no." Tarona went on to explain that French divers and teachers on the atoll for work kept the house occupied as a long-term rental.

During those ten years, we hopped around, staying here and there. Each place we stayed was nice enough, and each place had us meeting new people and slowly widening our circle of friends, but we were always dreaming of returning to the shack in the sand. We'd pass by on our bikes and stop on the side of the road to longingly gaze at it. We'd pass by in our boat and slow down and stare some more. We'd stop in every now and then to visit Tarona and her husband, Moana, to find out what was new with them. Year after year, we never stopped dreaming, dreaming, dreaming of living in that house once again.

We accumulated a lot of stuff during those years: two bicycles, two big boxes of atoll gear, and, finally, a boat. I had also found a dear friend, Scarlett, the only other expat American woman here. In between our regular stays, Scarlett and her husband, Rich, kindly kept our bikes and gear under their house. Teiva and Meho kept our boat in their yard.

At one point during those ten years, we even considered building our own house. Land, clear and free, was offered to us. It was so tempting. The lot sat on the lagoon, was remote, and was already leveled and ready for construction. Did I mention that it was beautiful? After giving it some serious thought, we decided we were too old to do battle with a myriad of French regulations that would most certainly be ahead of us with a construction project like that. Naturally, I had already drawn up a rough set of plans, picked the materials, and consulted with a builder out of Pape'ete.

After giving up on the idea of building, I put out my feelers to everyone we knew in Rangiroa. We were looking for a long-term house rental. We decided that a five-year stint should cure us of our itch to be here. During my quest, I called Tarona again, just to be sure the shack in the sand was still occupied by long-term renters. A real miracle occurred. The French divers who were currently living in the house were moving on, and we could have it once again. We fine-tuned an arrangement with Tarona and Moana, and that was that. We are in the fourth year of our lease, and already we are not sure if we will be ready to give this place up. It truly is a dream come true.

— POSTSCRIPT —

Le Sauvage closed after several years of operation. Many people, including us, were heartbroken. It's sitting empty now. The fares *are deteriorating, and everything is returning to nature. There is just a caretaker living out there now. I've heard talk of it being renovated and reopened. From what I understand of the plans, it will be an upscale* motu *with all the bells and whistles for today's discriminating and very well-to-do traveler. While I'll try not to be too opinionated here, I'll take the old Sauvage with the kerosene lanterns any day.*

Sadly, Raimana, the gentle giant of a Tahitian man from our Le Sauvage days, passed away. Whenever we hear the word "WOW," we say his name. It was one of the few English words he knew. We visited his resting spot in the Tiputa Village cemetery and left a lei that said, "Ta'oto maita'i" *(sleep well). We think of him often, and we miss him.*

That beautiful lot that we almost purchased down the way is still empty. It was sold to a Swiss woman. We slow down our boat every time we pass. I always envision the little house that I designed sitting there on the property. Then I picture the two of us sitting right there on the lanai with our feet propped up, gazing out at this incredible lagoon.

I consider that beautiful, young vahine *who told us of Tarona and Moana's house to be our guardian angel. I told her so and why. She led us to this spot, and she will forever be special to us. She's just moved to France. I can't believe that she'd leave this place.*

OUR "SHACK" IN THE SAND

Yesterday, I read the previous chapter aloud to Scooter. When I was done, he asked me, "Why do you call this house a shack?" Hmm, I thought. "I'm not sure," I answered. We talked about it, and we agreed: This is actually a very nice house. It is not a shack.

There is a nice kitchen with a full-size refrigerator/freezer, a small four-burner stove/oven (powered by a *gaz* bottle located just outside), a microwave, and a double sink. The kitchen cabinets are Tahitian style, with no cabinet doors, just curtains. There are bifold doors across the front of the house facing the lagoon. The entire wall opens up with those bifold doors, making the house completely open to the lagoon. They stay open all day, making it feel like we're basically outside. A teak dining table that Scooter refinished, accompanied by four colorful chairs, takes up residence in the kitchen.

Our lanai, which serves as our living room, perches in front of the kitchen. It's covered by a new thatch roof that does not leak unless there's a massive downpour. There is a cocktail table, four chairs, and a compact high-top bar. One step down from the lanai, and you're in the sand.

Behind the kitchen, there is a step up into an elevated bedroom/sitting area. Pocket doors that slide into the walls are always open during the day. We've got a large, comfy bed, and there's a dresser that acts as our "office." There's a media corner with all our electronics, a library/game corner, and the last corner has open shelving with containers to hold our clothes. A small sofa and coffee table are at the foot of the bed. We seldom use the mini sofa unless there's a huge storm raging, and we can't go outside. Last but not least, an AC unit is wall-mounted just above the bed. AC is not essential here, but it sure makes for pleasant nights.

Behind the bedroom is a step down into the bathroom/laundry room. There's a brand-new washing machine, a free-standing sink, and a nicely tiled shower with a hot-water-on-demand unit fueled by another *gaz* bottle outside. This room appears to be scaled for giants. The mirror and towel hooks are placed high up on the walls. If you're not a giant, you need to take a short hop up to see yourself or to hang a towel.

An exterior flight of stairs leads to the second floor. The upstairs serves as Scooter's "man cave," housing his tools, boat equipment, bicycle spare parts, and just about everything else guys like. His friends come over, look around, and drool. The guys have named the upstairs "The Chinese Store" due to the sheer volume and variety of cool stuff. This area has potential to become a second bedroom, but I know better than to invade his space.

There's a large carport running along the entire west side of the house. It has become an additional room since we closed off the entry end with a bamboo gate. The carport also faces the lagoon. There is a large picnic table that seats ten. This is where we have dinner parties at night and where we do our projects during the day. There's a big exterior closet in the carport that we call "ACE Hardware." Inside ACE are tools, art supplies, snorkel gear, paint and brushes, gardening equipment, and everything else we need to keep a house running smoothly. Our bikes, Vespa, and e-bike are all parked in the carport. We hang laundry up to dry under the corrugated tin roof in this area as well.

The house is an A-frame design. It looks very Polynesian because of a few trim details and the thatch roof over the lanai. The house is built of wood with Masonite siding painted a pleasant light tan color. It's high-quality construction, both inside and out. The steep angle of the roof helps us capture water in the two large catchment tanks in the side yard to the east. Windows are glass louvers in the bedroom and bathroom, and traditional Tahitian prop ups in the kitchen. We have a front door, but nobody uses it, preferring to walk through the carport to the beachside lanai.

The house is about 450 square feet, and the lanai is an additional 120 square feet. With the addition of the carport and the Chinese Store upstairs, the overall square footage is about fourteen hundred. We use every square foot for something. We don't feel cramped at all; in fact, it feels just right.

Electricity is provided by the Commune de Rangiroa's generating plant. A system called Cash Power works in concert with the power plant. We have a small box in the bedroom that tells us how much power we currently have on hand. If it's getting low, we ride six miles into Avatoru Village to buy more power units at a local store, Magasin Chez Daniel. We can only pay in cash. When we're done paying, the cashier gives us a receipt with a very long number. We come home and enter that long number on the keypad of the little box in the bedroom, and—voilà—more power.

Except for furniture, we have lugged all the household accessories we've needed from Hawaii over the past four years. You name it, and we have brought it. We have packed and hauled everything from an Instant Pot and salad spinner to ice cube trays and a toaster. We had several large-format art canvases printed up using photos of Tahiti. We rolled them all up with stretcher bars and a staple gun and brought them down in a big fishing rod travel tube.

We try to find things that use solar energy or that can be charged with iPhone cords, but most of all, we search out items that are light in weight. Packing our luggage has become a pure science. Each bag is exactly at the weight limit of fifty-one pounds. With four bags allowed and two carry-ons each, we estimate that we haul at least three hundred pounds each trip.

Scooter and I sometimes try to name the top ten things we have brought from Kona. It's hard because so many things have been exceptionally useful; other things make this place feel like home, and other things just make life more fun. When we're here in our paradise, we make lists upon lists, then divide and conquer for shopping duty while back in Hawaii. Scooter is an online shopper. He usually finds technical goodies on the Internet. I buy dry goods, housewares, and miscellaneous items around Kona.

Ever so slowly, this place has become a functional and comfortable home. There's not much more that we need. Our ultimate goal is to someday board a flight with just a small carry-on with transit essentials. We haven't gotten there yet, and chances are we never will.

One day a while back, I had a strange thing happen to me. It was a quiet, calm atoll morning. Scooter was off on the e-bike hunting for fresh fruits and vegetables in the village. I was all alone on our beach, methodically raking sand, minding my own business. It was sweltering hot, as usual. I momentarily stopped in the shade of the *tou* tree to take a breather and a quick sip of iced tea. I leaned on my rake and gazed back to our shack in the sand with no particular preconceived thoughts. As I stood there, surveying our personal little Tahitian paradise, I froze in place. I used just my eyes to scan the house, the yard, the beach. Otherwise, I could not move any other muscles. I was totally captivated as I looked at the vision before me, of what we had created with our hard work and determination. At that exact moment, I realized that my long-held dream of living in Tahiti in a house exactly like this had finally come true. Hot tears of pure joy welled up in my eyes. After a few minutes, I shook myself back to reality and got back to raking. I decided right then and there that dreams do, and can, come true, and this magical house, and our life on the atoll was proof enough for me.

— *POSTSCRIPT* —

Scooter is an excellent mechanic. I can dream things up, but am usually unable to fabricate them. Neither one of us is a carpenter. Building our new gate was a real experience. Our lack of building skills combined with very limited resources available on the atoll made the job seem impossible. The fact that our new gate is functional, balanced, works, and looks good is a miracle.

As with any house, there are hiccups with its ongoing operation. We have had our fair share of those: an AC meltdown, a water pump malfunction, leaking pipes under the sink and at the outdoor shower, a washing machine freakout, and on and on. When this happens, we try to fix things ourselves. Scooter has the tools and know-how. I lend support, hand him the tools, and hold the flashlight. If things are beyond our capabilities, we call Pierre, the Barefoot Plumber. When we work with Pierre and his vahine, *Poe, it is straight out of a scene with Lucy, Desi, Fred, and Ethel on the old* I Love Lucy *show. Pierre speaks no English. We speak little French, so Poe and I are left to speak Tahitian, trying to relay messages between Pierre and Scooter. At first, we were sure Pierre dreaded coming here to fix things because it was such a crazy three-ring circus created by the language barrier. Each time they left, we were exhausted. I'm sure they were, too. We think we may have finally won him over. The solution? A few cold Hinanos at the end of a repair project. No language is necessary to enjoy a cold beer. I've been told that Pierre, the Barefoot Plumber, was a French rock star back in the day.*

Learning to operate the new washing machine was an experience. I'm not very technical, and

I've never been one to read all the instructions that come with appliances. But when instructions are in French, neither one of us has a clue. Thankfully, our neighbor at the time, Eve, came over to translate the functions of all the flashing buttons on the washer. We got it running, but when we were back in Kona, we went online to print out the appliance booklet in English.

MRS. TETUANUI, TA'AROA, AND TAHI

After going up and down the road and up and down the lagoon, we decided that this neighborhood, the area where our shack in the sand is, was our favorite. It's sparsely populated, and there are a number of interesting neighbors.

On this piece of property, which we have named "Moana's Village," there are three nice houses and one *fare pote'e* that is used as a house. The houses are carefully situated so that there's quite a bit of privacy. All the houses are of similar design (A-frame, two-story), and all are painted light tan. The *fare pote'e* is a cluster of three small structures in the shape of a U facing the lagoon. There's a kitchen/bathroom pod, a sleeping pod, and a huge thatched open-air hut (*fare pote'e*) used as the living room. We all share a sandy driveway that leads in from the road and ends at our place on the lagoon. There's a nice garden, coconut trees, and a few places to park on the grass.

To the east and to the west, there is nothing except a thick coconut forest. To the south are the lagoon and lagoon beach. To the north, across the road, is the community flower garden where *tiare* flowers bloom for all to use in lei making. Beyond that is the reef beach and the pounding surf of the Pacific Ocean. To me, it feels like Moana's Village is a little island in and of itself since there are no immediate neighbors in any direction.

Our closest neighbor is on the lagoon side of the road, about a quarter mile away. Mrs. Tetuanui's house fronts the road. Her lush property stretches all the way to the lagoon. The house is older and has carved trim in Polynesian designs. There's a huge, old tractor tire by the road with TETUANUI neatly printed on it in white, capital letters. I believe that she is a widow, as I've never seen or met a Mr. Tetuanui. There are other occupants there at various times, although I don't know any of them or how they are related.

Mrs. Tetuanui makes leis. Almost every morning, she walks through the community flower garden, carefully picking only the very best *tiare* flowers. I'm up before dawn and out on the road to go for a run. I've gotten to know her since we're the only two people usually around at that hour. I greet her in Tahitian and wish her a good day. After a year or so, we began to stop and talk a bit about the weather, the beauty of her yard, or the pink sunrise we both noticed over the tops of the coconut trees. At first, I thought she might not really like me, a *popa'a* (foreigner). Lately, though, she smiles and laughs when we see each other and have our short, predawn chats. A few days ago, I was very happily surprised when she blew me a kiss as we parted ways. I'm mindful to always speak Tahitian with her, although sometimes she replies in French. Just recently I asked her if she would make two leis for me in June. I explained that it was for two friends' birthdays. We agreed on the price and roughed out a plan for when the time came. For some reason, I am drawn to Mrs. Tetuanui. To me, she represents the essence of a Polynesian *vahine*: kind, humble, and welcoming. I'm so glad that we are getting to know each other.

In the other direction, on the lagoon side of the road, just after the coconut forest, is Ta'aroa's cluster of houses. Ta'aroa and his wife, Elodie, live there with an assortment of kids, grandkids, dogs, and chickens. Ta'aroa is a giant of a man. He's a retired *gendarme*. He is also a drummer and chief of a dance troupe. Having a Tahitian drummer just down the road is such a pleasure. The beat of the *to'ere* and *pahu* drums stirs me to my core every time I'm lucky enough to hear them.

We went to a baby luau at Ta'aroa's about a year ago. They are such nice people: down to earth, full of life, and happy to share. A few days after that gathering, we saw a group of teenagers take off in a boat from his beach. We saw that one *vahine* was holding an infant. It looked like they were off to the *motu* to party. Just in front of our place their engine sputtered and died. The boat began to drift aimlessly. Scooter didn't hesitate for a minute. He jumped up and into our boat and quickly got out there to give them a tow back to Ta'aroa's beach. They were so thankful, especially the *vahine* with the baby. From that point on, the entire family waves and shouts *'iaorana* to us every time they pass by.

Ta'aroa has a fleet of colorful kayaks; no two are the same color. On the weekends or after school, a flotilla of kids and dogs paddle past our place in a race to the *hoa* just down by Mrs. Tetuanui's house. Hours later, after playing in the *hoa*, they all paddle back to Ta'aroa's beach, each colorful kayak moving a little slower than during the lively race down.

Recently, the family built a little takeout food stand by the road. They prepare chicken and fries or steak and fries in their kitchen, then walk the food out to the booth to sell from the roadside. Their business was going like gangbusters for quite a while, with cars coming and going. The booth is still there; however, we haven't seen any sign of Tahitian takeout lately.

Almost every day around noon, we see Ta'aroa and Elodie out in the lagoon, soaking quietly in the liquid, turquoise warmth. We are out there too, sometimes. We always wave to each other. I can't see that far, but I hope that they are smiling like we are.

Across the street from Ta'aroa, just next door to the community flower garden, is Tahi. Tahi is a carver. He has waist-length gray dreadlocks and rides a motorcycle. He was an art teacher at the local trade school, teaching junior high kids to carve pearl shell, bone, and local hardwood. Recently he went to France to teach there. He was gone for about a year. Now he's back tap, tap, tapping away all day long inside his house. I love the sound. I have yet to see his work. By all accounts, he is a master carver and quite famous throughout Tahiti.

There is some connection between Tahi and Mrs. Tetuanui. I asked Teiva about it, and he didn't know. Maybe they are brother and sister. Maybe they are cousins. Maybe they are just old friends. They are often at each other's house or talking story in the flower garden. They seem to share a pack of docile dogs that live at one house, then the other. Just this morning, when I ran past, they were walking together, talking quietly as they headed toward Mrs. Tetuanui's house. It was just getting light out.

Becoming a part of this neighborhood has been a slow process. It has taken its sweet time for us to ease into conversations and interact with the neighbors. Speaking my rudimentary Tahitian has greatly helped. Scooter's boating and fishing skills have also helped. Locals can be wary of *popa'as*, and with good reason. A place this beautiful gets eaten alive by foreigners who want a piece of it for themselves. We know and will never forget that we are just guests here for a few fleeting years.

MY OUT-OF-CONTROL, CRAZY OBSESSION

I'm not sure how this whole thing started. It's something that I certainly did not plan. It just happened. If I had planned this, you'd really have to call me crazy. I'm referring to my obsession with creating a beach of only pure, soft sand.

There's more sand on a coral atoll than anyone can imagine. Mixed in with all the sand are chunks of coral. Big chunks, little chunks, minute chunks, white chunks, pink chunks, gray chunks, and every kind of chunk. Some chunks of coral are beautiful and shaped like a head of cauliflower. Some are shaped like hearts, slim cigarettes, the letter Y, and chicken feet. Many chunks are very old and worn down with little texture. The newer ones have very sharp nodules that can easily cut your fingertips. Some chunks just look like nondescript rocks. Huge chunks, or shelves of coral called *papa*, serve as the base of the atoll. I know all about coral chunks because

I've spent more than three years slowly sifting them out of the sand on our beach.

This morning on my iPad, a photo randomly popped up. We had taken it in March of 2019, the month we had moved in here. The photo shows our beach. Scooter and I were both shocked when we looked at the picture a bit closer. I can see in the photo that I have started to line the yard with coconuts. The beach, at that time, could accurately be called "coral rubble." We were shocked because our beach looks nothing like that these days. We had forgotten the shabby shape it was in upon our arrival.

If I recall correctly, the first month we were here, I looked out and saw a big, ugly barbeque grill, which had been left smack dab in the middle of our beach by the previous tenants. It was black with the soot of burned branches and had several broken cement blocks positioned to hold aloft the rusty grill. It was an eyesore. I guess I thought to myself, "Hey, I'll clean up this area. It will just take a few hours." And so my obsession began.

I had a rusty old rake, a wheelbarrow with a flat tire, and a blue dustpan that I brought down from Kona. I don't recall how I sifted the sand early on. Maybe I just raked and raked and made a pile of the larger pieces of coral in a corner of the yard. I must have thought, "I'm going to need something to sift this sand a bit," still not knowing at that point what obsession lay ahead of me.

The next trip down I brought two white, decorative mesh

baskets I found on the sale rack at the Kona Target. They measured about twelve by twelve inches and cost ninety-nine cents each. I began at one end of the beach and scraped, then scooped the rubble with the blue dustpan into a mesh basket. I used that dustpan to dig a few inches down into the coral rubble. As I sifted, nice sand was left behind, and the coral chunks were left in the mesh basket. I dumped the chunks from the basket into the wheelbarrow and carted it off into the coconut forest. I worked every morning after breakfast. I would set a goal each day of maybe one foot. So, one foot at a time, I progressed along our beach. It looked better immediately, and that motivated me to continue. My goal was to make it to the end of our beach.

The next trip I brought a roll of mesh that I bought at Lowe's. It was big enough to staple to two pieces of scrap wood we found in Moana's garage. The mesh frame we constructed fit perfectly over the wheelbarrow. Miraculously, Moana had replaced the flat tire on the wheelbarrow by then. As before, I worked every morning. Moving toward the end of the beach went faster because of the larger size of the receiving container, the wheelbarrow. When I finally reached the edge of the beach, instead of stopping, as I had planned, I began to sift up toward the house and then, after that, down toward the lagoon, widening the patch of freshly sifted sand.

Pretty soon I realized that I could move sand around. The side yard was deep with drifts of nice, white sand. I must have reasoned to myself, "Why not sift that nice sand and move it onto the main beach where it would be appreciated more? Who cares about the side yard anyway?" After I moved most of the sand from the side yard, I began to hunt for more deep pockets of sand in our yard. None were left, so a whole new stage began: sand importation.

Looking back, I can see now that this was when the sand obsession kicked into high gear. I really didn't need any more sand. Our yard was finally sandy, beautiful, and coral free. I simply wanted more sand. I wanted to make our beach deeper and deeper and softer and softer with pristine, golden sand. I started looking down at the beach in front of the coconut forest. After storms or an exceptionally high tide, beautiful pockets of squeaky-clean sand would magically appear as if just for me. I'd head down with my ragtag collection of tools and wobble back with full wheelbarrow loads of sparkling sand. It was hard, sweltering work. I had to limit myself to three wheelbarrow trips a day. At one point, Scooter had to jump in to help transport the sand. We have a set of walkie-talkies. I'd take mine down the beach and call back when the wheelbarrow was almost overflowing, saying something like, "Got a full load, Scooter. Over." "Copy," he'd reply. Down he'd come and power that wheelbarrow back and spread the new layer of sand out like nobody's business.

It's now our fourth year here, and I believe that I have reached the final stage of my sand obsession: maintenance. My morning is now spent raking leaves and grooming the sand, although I have a confession. Last week a big pocket of sand appeared down the way, and I couldn't help myself. Three days and nine more wheelbarrow loads later, it created a fluffy new topcoat on our beach.

The new French neighbors here at Moana's Village have silently watched my madness while comfortably seated in their beach chairs down by Ta'aroa's. Surely, they have all asked each other what's up with the crazy American woman and her wire basket and blue dustpan? William, the mellow Tahitian next door in the *fare pote'e*, just smiles at me and my rake and goes back to swimming in the languid lagoon.

Teiva has named our beach Waikiki. The other day, he reminded me of something I already knew: one hurricane could arrive tomorrow, and all of the golden sand would be inside our house. Knowing and remembering that fact will, hopefully, temper my mad obsession.

— *POSTSCRIPT*

That blue dustpan gets the Vahine *Seal of Approval. It's amazing that, considering all that I have put it through, it's still pristine and without a chip or scratch. The ninety-nine-cent mesh baskets are rusted and bent, but still in use daily. The rusty, old rake never wavered or broke. The wheelbarrow, which is owned by*

Moana, has been commandeered by one of the new neighbors. It's parked majestically in his garage. Now, when I want to use it, I ask him politely, using gestures and my fractured French, if I might borrow the brouette *(wheelbarrow, in French) for an hour or so. He has no idea what that wheelbarrow and I have gone through.*

Moana and Tarona moved to Pape'ete. He is the liaison for the Commune de Rangiroa. He returns to the atoll often for work. He always stops in to say hello, share a cold drink, and talk story on our lanai. He is very happy about the beach sand. In fact, his eyes pop out every time he surveys his property. He was curious about how I did it. I explained the whole thing. He was pretty much amazed. When we got the chance to move back in here, I made a list of things we would do as good tenants. One item on that list promised that we would care for their house and yard as if it were our own. We have kept that promise, and then some.

While relocating all the chunks of coral to the coconut forest, I began to wonder if I could use them somehow in our yard. Just recently, I started creating areas of chunked coral behind the lines of coconut yard trim to create a visual contrast to the soft, pure sand. It looks great. A bit later, I began to use the chunks to "repave" our driveway.

OUR BIGGEST CHALLENGE

We have been blessed to live in the US where fresh, bountiful food is readily available. You can pop into any market at any time of day, on any day of the week, and find what you want and need. Abundance reigns supreme in the American food supply realm. I have never given this notion much thought—that is until we began to live on a coral atoll.

In Rangiroa, food is scarce. Obtaining food, meaning fresh fruits and vegetables, is almost a full-time job. It takes planning and time to fill your refrigerator with what you need. This has been our biggest challenge. The learning curve is steep, and climbing up that hill has been a snail-paced journey. Living here is full of challenges, some big and some small. Obtaining food to eat is more than a challenge. It is a basic need that must be met for survival.

Normally Scooter and I are healthy eaters. Let me rephrase

that: We are healthy eaters in Kona. It took us a while to come to the realization that we just had to let go of some of our healthy eating habits while on the atoll. We had to figure out how to eat as healthfully as possible with a very limited food supply. We have learned, and we have adapted. We had to.

The first thing that had to sink into our brains was that food, in general, does not grow here. Plants and trees generally need soil to thrive. We live on coral and sand. There are a few hardy exceptions: banana palms, papaya trees, fig trees, and breadfruit trees. I have heard that watermelons grow out on the *motu*. Grapes also grow very well here; in fact, there is a vineyard out on a *motu* to the west. A few people attempt vegetable gardening. Doing that requires shipping huge bags of soil from Pape'ete. These hardy souls use sheets of corrugated metal roofing to "hug" their garden rows so that the precious soil does not migrate out into the surrounding sand. I grow microgreens hydroponically on our lanai in a small container. I harvest one mini-crop each week. That's the limit of our gardening efforts. With our constant coming and going, it's impossible for us to grow any vegetables, even if we import soil and plant seeds as soon as we arrive. The timing is just not right to plant and harvest within a three-month time span. I have just spread some papaya seeds in a small, contained patch of imported soil. Let's see what happens.

One key to getting food is understanding the cargo ships and their various schedules. The cargo ships bring food. There are four cargo ships that call at Rangiroa. They come from

Pape'ete or the Marquesas and stop at several atolls on their semiregular route. While there is a schedule, the ships may or may not stick to that schedule. They might break down along the way. They might run aground on a reef. They might not arrive at all if they are in dry dock for repair. There could be a storm, severe wind, or other natural occurrence that holds things up. The captains of two ships vying for dock space might get into a fist fight and delay the unloading process. Nobody knows exactly what's happening when it comes to the arrival of food.

When, and if, a cargo ship gets here, it pulls into one of three docks. Which dock at what time? It's a guessing game. We have learned to look down the lagoon with our binoculars, listen for a loud horn blast from the captain announcing his arrival, observe the direction of road traffic, and tune in to the coconut wireless (the informal sharing of news). Thankfully, friends call or text us if they know more in the main village than we do out here at the far end. Even though everyone is waiting for fresh food, it's a common courtesy to notify others of any information regarding food availability.

Another big factor in getting food is figuring out when you think each store will get the fresh items out on their shelves after delivery from the cargo ships. Seven small stores, called *magasins*, are scattered all along a six-mile stretch of road. The average size of a store is equivalent to a two-car garage. All stores open very early in the morning. Most close at midday for a few hours, then reopen and remain open until around six in the evening. Inside each *magasin*, you will see everything from bicycles to lawnmowers to bars of chocolate and boxes of matches. I'd estimate that only 1 percent (or less) of all the items in a store consist of fresh fruits and vegetables. Fresh is a relative term anyway since it has all been sitting inside a cargo hold for several days while getting here. If you do not get to the store as soon as the "freshies" (fresh fruits and vegetables) are put out, you are simply out of luck. It will be a wait until another ship pulls in, and all that you will see for sale are shrunken potatoes, blackened carrots, and a few soft yellow onions.

Another thing to learn is which store carries which items. Scooter has been doing all our shopping since he commands the e-bike, which now has two large shopping baskets attached. He knows which stores have what, and he's learning to ask if he doesn't see something. It's a long way to the best store. Before we had the e-bike, it was peddle, peddle, peddle all the way there, only to find the shelves empty. Now he can cruise around looking for what we need, hitting several stores on one trip into the village and make it back in time to recharge the bike.

We have adapted by bringing food items down that complement what is available here. That includes things like seasoning packets for stir fries, curry cubes, Mexican spices, and a wide variety of sauce mixes. We're learning to modify recipes by substituting ingredients with something similar that can be found here. I'm getting better at cooking breadfruit in different ways and using coconut milk as an ingredient. Recently, we discovered a nice, grainy "toasting bread" from New Zealand, and corn on the cob in the freezer section. Now we're really living!

We've brought down cooking equipment that has helped us broaden our capabilities to make a wider variety of food. We've hauled an Instant Pot, a tortilla press, a handheld blender, and a two-slice toaster, in addition to all the basic kitchen equipment.

It's part of the culture here to share and trade food and to give food as gifts. We love trading fish that we've caught for papaya, mango, or breadfruit. We trade regularly with all our friends and neighbors. Trading is at its peak just after the *Aranui* has called in to deliver fresh fruit from the Marquesas. My microgreens have been a big hit, as lettuce is almost nonexistent. People love them, or so they tell me. I make sure to always have a lot on hand to barter out or just give away.

We have found that because food is so precious, we are way more careful with it than normal. We store it carefully, use every morsel, do not overbuy, and plan meals using the ripest items first. There's very little waste around here, and if we must throw out overripe food, we do so with great sorrow.

At the end of our first extended stay, we decided that everything had gone well. At that time, we agreed that, moving forward, food was going to be our biggest challenge and our priority to address. While it had really been a good stay, a tinge of melancholy set in at the end because we weren't satisfied with what we were able to eat. The next trip was immensely better, and our efforts have constantly improved since then. We have had to learn, change, adapt, and be creative.

Looking about as I type away on my iPad, I see green bananas hanging up to ripen under our thatched lanai and large, shiny-skinned mangoes in the fruit bowl on the kitchen table, both fresh off the *Aranui* from the Marquesas. Also in my sight: a tray of microgreens just about ready for harvest. We've had two cargo ships this week. Things are looking up. *Tama'a maita'i*! (Eat well.)

WIND, WEATHER, AND STORMS

Many years ago we had a harrowing boat ride in this vast lagoon. It was such an intense experience that I can still remember it as if it happened just yesterday. Scooter and I occasionally talk about the incident and always with a shudder. This occurred way, way before we made it our business to learn about wind, weather, and storms in these waters.

We were out at Le Sauvage on a distant *motu*. After a beautiful evening of food and friendship in the communal dining area, we took our lantern and headed back to our *fare* way down the beach. On the silent walk, we looked up. We were in awe of the brilliant sky. It was almost totally white with stars. There was not a breath of wind.

We were awakened a few hours later by a violent wind shaking our *fare*. Relentless gusts blew right through the woven walls. The thud, thud, thud of falling coconuts echoed all around us. We lay there, wide awake, wondering if coconut trees would fall through the thatch roof. The wind screeched, something I'd never heard before or since. It was a long, sleepless night.

We were due to depart from the *motu* the next morning, a Saturday. We were scheduled to fly back to Pape'ete on Saturday afternoon, catch our midnight flight to Honolulu, and catch the first flight back to Kona on Sunday morning. I had work on Monday, and nothing could go wrong with the plan.

A dark, gray morning dawned. The normally placid lagoon was whipped into a crazed, ugly frenzy the color of chocolate milk. The wind continued to howl, and rain pelted us with stinging drops that pierced our faces. We had to scream to be heard when standing only a foot away from each other. It wasn't looking like I'd be making it back to work on Monday.

We were thinking that we'd be marooned out there with just a few other castaways for who knows how long. Just as we were mentally making plans to hunker down, we were surprised to see a boat emerge from the watery chaos. The driver pulled his skiff up on the beach. He jumped out, shook himself off, then ran inside the dining *fare* for a hot cup of coffee. That boat was to be our transport back to the village. I guess we wouldn't be stuck on Gilligan's Island after all. We packed up our backpacks, put on oversize rain gear, and, against our better judgment, hopped in the boat with the driver. It was just the three of us.

I'd never held on to a boat so tightly. My fingers ached,

and my body, infused with fear, was totally rigid. Scooter, a seasoned boat captain, was not his usual laid-back self. His jaw was set, and I noticed he had white knuckles, too. It was the longest boat ride of my life. It got even worse when, in the middle of the lagoon, the driver told us through the pelting rain that he was the local pizza maker who was merely filling in for the regular shuttle boat guy. We made it back to the village, and, of course, the day cleared up just after we tied up at the dock. The lagoon became picture postcard perfect once again. It was as if that storm had never happened.

These days we are hypersensitive to the weather nuances around us. If the wind subtly changes direction, we notice and comment. If a wave breaks from a new angle, we watch with our eyes glued to the lagoon. If black clouds are approaching from the east, we get ready for rain and pull in laundry from the line. If the boat swings around on its mooring, we are poised to move, if necessary, to untangle ropes, chains, and anchors. We are always watching, watching, watching the weather. Our house is open all day, every day, to the elements. We notice everything and feel changes, even while we are just sitting at the dining table eating our morning toast.

We have learned about the different winds and what to expect when they suddenly arrive. The worst wind for us is the *mara'amu*, from the southeast. It blows directly into our house. It travels across the lagoon and picks up moisture, which ends up in our kitchen. Waves jump up in height and break with force. Some waves are sizable and shocking as they march onward, right toward us. We find ourselves continually yelling, "Look at this one!" from our lanai as increasingly bigger sets approach. A *mara'amu* can last for days, sometimes weeks. Everything is wet, salty, and wind tattered. It can be tiring and scary. The sounds of our boat bucking like a wild bronco kept us awake many long nights as it rode out a *mara'amu*. Listening to the wind and waves had me doing boat checks with a flashlight. Sleepless nights get old, fast.

One morning I was busy in the kitchen trying to master the art of making nonfat vanilla yogurt. My Kona surf pal, Olivia, had assured me that it was very easy. She even gave me her extra cooking thermometer for my atoll kitchen, which is essential for one step in the process. Timing and temperature are critical to successful yogurt making. Just at the critical moment of my scientific cooking experiment, a *mara'amu* blew into the kitchen with such sudden force that it hurled several wine glasses onto the floor. Picture this scene: I'm trying to watch the timer, monitor the red line on the thermometer, not step in broken glass, and keep an eye out on our boat that was rearing against her mooring ropes and chains. It was like a three-ring circus, and I was the frazzled clown in the center ring.

Scooter goes online regularly to Windy.com to see what's in the forecast. Teiva uses a website called Windguru. He calls us if he sees something on his site that we might not see on ours. As soon as we hear a *mara'amu* is on the way, we

Mom and Dad's California wedding, 1945

Brice, Stephanie, and Carol in the paddle wheel boat

Dad diving off of his canoe—Puna'auia

Mom on the main drag, Uturoa, Raiatea

A movie still of Dad as a mutineer in *Mutiny on the Bounty*, Pape'ete

Finding my atoll—Rangiroa

Our first trip to Le Sauvage

Where we found perfection—Le Sauvage

Looking out from our shack in the sand

Looking at our shack in the sand

Scooter and I under the thatch

"Numba one sand sifttah"

Bananas arrive on the *Aranui*

Ripening bananas, mangoes, and a tray of microgreens

The Shoppingmobile

My custom Tahitian wind rose pillow made by Scarlett

Vahine Iti at our favorite picnic spot

Exploring the atoll in *Vahine Iti*

The day before *Vahine Iti* crashed on the reef

Scooter "MacGyver" Fuller with painting gear

The *hoa* in March with circling black tips

Catching lagoon fish

Catching big game fish

The little nemesis of a radio

After the XXXL Storm of the Century

3D drying by Carol

Our "ghost"

Custom Weber barbecue by Scooter

Marine debris art—"The Yellow Submarine"

I'a pehu, "Trash Fish"

Motu Mahuta

Carol and Jillyn finally meet in Rangiroa

close down the house, and the boat goes to the *hoa* for safety. Once there, Scooter ties it off fore and aft with heavy lines to a few strong coconut trees. Having it moored just out front is great; however, knowing that it's safe in bad weather is so much better, plus we get a good night's sleep.

Winds out of the north are called *to'erau*. They are cold (relatively speaking) winds. We are protected from their fury. People living on the outer reef take the brunt of this wind. Here on the lagoon side, it's peaceful all along the shore. A short distance out into the lagoon, where it's out of the lee of the land, the *to'erau* wreaks havoc.

Most days the prevailing wind, *maoa'e,* blows steadily from east to west. This wind blows sideways past our house and continues down our *motu*. The coconut forest usually protects us from this wind. It can be fierce at times, and if the angle slightly changes, making it blow more to the south, it can cause problems like the *mara'amu*.

Days with no wind at all are rare. They are so beautiful, but then the flies and mosquitoes arrive. If the totally calm spell goes on for several days, soon we're asking each other, "When will we get a puff of wind again?" After a long spell of totally still days, the wind isn't sure what it wants to do. Teiva told us about this and warned us to be careful because anything can, and does, happen. That is exactly what happened about six months ago. After a long, calm spell, a *mara'amu* and a *to'erau* arrived all at once. The powerful north and south swells collided with each other and created humongous waves. It was very early in the morning when this freak storm arrived. We were up and alert. We watched helplessly from our lanai as our boat jumped its mooring and, within seconds, crashed into the reef in front of our next-door neighbor, William's, *fare pote'e*. It was shocking, but we had no time to feel sorry for ourselves. We got people and equipment here to help save her. By noon, she was back in our carport, waterlogged, bashed, and battered.

Given how important they are to our daily lives, I'm trying to become familiar with the name of each wind direction. We listen to the weather reports on the radio, and knowing the various weather terms is essential to understanding what to expect and what to prepare for. Scarlett made me a pillow one year for my birthday. It has the Tahitian wind rose on it. That pillow, while beautiful and decorative, has become a tool for us. We refer to it when listening to the weatherman.

Both Scooter and I are water people. He's had more than forty-five years on the ocean as a boat captain, plus an additional four years in the US Navy. I've had almost forty years of experience in the water, surfing. Nothing can humble us like the power of the ocean. We respect its ferocity and are in awe of its beauty. We never get complacent, especially here in the Tuamotus.

— POSTSCRIPT —

The "pizza guy" is still here making pizza. He's got a takeout business operating from the back door of his house in Ohotu Village. It's a tasty pizza. Scooter and I agree; he did a good job of keeping us alive that stormy day, and he's a great pizza maker.

The next chapter will tell you all about our boat, Vahine Iti. *There will be more about the disastrous crash on the reef during that morning of the perfect storm.*

I have never learned to make nonfat vanilla yogurt successfully.

VAHINE ITI

I had no idea we would ever own a boat in Tahiti. Just living in French Polynesia was a big enough dream for me. Now when we are skimming over the turquoise lagoon in *Vahine Iti*, my eyes sometimes well up with tears of pure joy. When I get misty eyed, Scooter knows why. He grabs my hand, pulls me over, and we hug each other tight. Here's the story of how we became the captain and deckhand on a snug little boat on a coral atoll. It's a bit of a meandering tale, with a few ups and a few downs. At the end of the roller-coaster ride, we're still very happy to be skimming along in the blue—together.

Having a boat has given us so much freedom. Freedom to be ourselves. Freedom to go where we want, do what we want, and decide when we want to do it. The flip side of that delicious freedom is accepting responsibility for our own safety, the safety of others, and the safety of our boat. Nobody is watching over us out there. The sea is an immense place that can have very serious consequences. With forty-five years on the ocean, Scooter has the credentials to handle most of what this place dishes out.

Long ago, we would rent little tin boats while vacationing on Bora Bora. These basic tin boats are called *faraipani* in Tahitian, "frying pans." Spending the day in our little boat was always an adventure. We found that we preferred to explore the Bora lagoon on our own as opposed to an organized excursion. We'd leave early in the morning, go all over that incredible turquoise water wonderland, and make it back just before sunset, and, yes, we were totally fried at the end of the day. A while later we rented a house, boat, and car on Huahine, another popular Tahitian island in the Iles Sous Vent area of French Polynesia. We never used the car, but we went everywhere in that frying pan. Once again, we found that we preferred the freedom of exploring the lagoon at our own pace, making our own adventures, and meeting people along the way.

Many years later, when we were bouncing around renting different places in Rangiroa, we happened upon a house that was for rent on a *motu* about three miles down from Tiputa Village. The setup sounded like a great match for us, so we booked a month with Tepu, the owner. We knew that we'd be happier there if we had a boat to make trips to the village for food and supplies. We ended up "renting" a frying pan from Tuaore, Meho's mother. It got us back and forth, but the outboard was finicky and difficult for Scooter to pull start. It also leaked, and was a very bumpy ride.

During that trip, we learned all about real Paumotu living—how people in the Tuamotus live. We hauled water, fuel, food, and supplies between the village and the house on Tepu's *motu*. It was time-consuming, hard, hot, and heavy work. We figured things out as we went and did a pretty good job of surviving. We returned Tuaore's boat in one piece and vowed to start looking around for a boat to buy for our next stay at Tepu's.

Back in Kona, we began our online search. At first, we thought about buying a frying pan in Pape'ete and having it shipped out to Rangiroa. After a bit of research, we became discouraged. The prices were outrageous. A few months later I saw an ad online on the Rangiroa Vente (Craigslist for Rangiroa) site. A boat was listed for sale. It looked just about right for us. It was sixteen feet long and had a Bimini top and a Suzuki 70 HP outboard motor. The owner, a French *gendarme* stationed in Rangiroa, was returning to France after his tour of duty in French Polynesia. Scooter and I looked at the photos and information, then we looked at each other, and then we called Teiva right away. Teiva and Meho went to check the boat out at the *gendarmerie*. They took it on a test run, emailed us a ton of pictures, and said that it looked "pretty good."

After a bit of haggling between Teiva and the *gendarme*, the deal was settled. We sent off a money transfer to France, and the boat was ours. Teiva and Meho towed the boat to their yard and kindly kept it there until our next trip. Scarlett helped, too, by emailing all the official forms to us with the translations into English. We completed the paperwork for the registration and snail-mailed it off to *des Affaires Maritimes* in Papeete. One of the questions on the forms asked if we'd like a new name for the boat. I had always said, "If I had a boat, I'd name her *Vahine*." Of course, I was imagining a sleek, dark-hulled schooner. That name would be perfect for such a classy vessel. Our boat definitely did not rate that name, so we decided on *Vahine Iti* (Little Girl). It was playful, and it fit.

On our next trip, we launched her, loaded up our gear, and headed straight back down to Tepu's *motu*. We used a rusty, old pole that was stuck in a coral head as our mooring and tied another rope to the sturdy tree just in front of our house. Tepu gave us instructions on what to do in case a *mara'amu* arrived. Thankfully, the weather cooperated for the entire month we were there. *Vahine Iti* greatly improved our treks to and from the village. She handled well and was comfortable. Having shade from the Bimini top was a game changer. Right off the bat, we knew that buying the boat had been a good move.

Scooter began to modify, upgrade, and fine-tune the boat almost as soon as we got it. Before we knew it, *Vahine Iti* was looking great and running like a top. He added a hydraulic steering system, repaired all the wires that were eaten by rats while in Teiva's yard, added new swivel seats, modified the Bimini top, added a fin to the outboard so she'd ride more efficiently, installed new rod holders, and on and on. Together we washed and waxed her, and soon she was a little showstopper.

After about two years of enjoying our boat, we still had not received anything official back from *des Affaires Maritimes*. Finally, a packet arrived. There was a bit of a problem. The letter stated that non-French citizens are not allowed to own a boat in French Polynesia. Really? Nobody we knew had ever heard of this rule, not even the French *gendarme* who sold it to us. So, we "sold" 51 percent of *Vahine Iti* to Teiva, retained ownership of the other 49 percent, and sent in the revised paperwork. That was how we played that little game. *'Aita pe'ape'a*, we said, no worries.

When we moved back into our shack in the sand, our top priority was figuring out a mooring for *Vahine Iti*. We had a big blue swimming hole a short distance out front, and it was deep enough to moor a boat. Teiva and Scooter set everything up, and, within a week, *Vahine Iti* was bobbing up and down tied off to a big orange mooring ball about twenty-five yards out. They rigged up chains, more chains, ropes, backup ropes, and backups for the backups. The system was secure enough to hold a battleship, or so we thought. Scooter set up a guide rope from the mooring ball to the shore so that he could back *Vahine Iti* right in for loading and fueling from the beach.

For the first few years, she stayed on her mooring out front, even during the *mara'amu*. After too many sleepless nights and a few close calls, Teiva helped us get a spot set up for her in the *hoa* just down the way. We'd take her down when a storm was expected and kept her there until the wind died back down. That worked well until the perfect storm arrived out of nowhere early one morning.

I took a photo of Scooter that shows him sitting on the lanai, looking out at *Vahine Iti*. We had just launched her. It was a beautiful, glassy day. He had worked on her for the entire previous week, applying two coats of bottom paint and fine-tuning various systems while she was still on the trailer. It's hard to believe, but within twenty-four hours of that photo, *Vahine Iti* was ripped from the mooring and smashed on the reef down the beach.

Out of nowhere, a *mara'amu* and a *to'erau* arrived together, creating monstrous waves—the biggest we'd ever seen in the lagoon. At about six in the morning after a calm night, the two forces hit with a sudden vengeance. We were both up and watching from the beach. It was so painful to watch the storm thrash *Vahine Iti*. She was rearing and bucking in the chaos. Scooter wanted to go out and get the motor going so that when (note: not if, but when) she broke free, he could get her away from the shore. I said, "No way." He would have been hurt or even killed. The waves lifted her so high that the chains and ropes just lifted straight up and off. We watched her go. It was shocking and heartbreaking. Within seconds, she hit the reef and landed on a coral shelf. With adrenaline pumping, we immediately tied her off to a tree to minimize the bashing from the incessant wave action.

Teiva appeared; then Rama (a longtime friend and fishing

buddy of Scooter's); then Terii, Teiva's son; and then a few other guys we didn't know. Somebody brought giant truck tires. Scooter had a come-along (winch) that helped immensely. We looked all over for logs or something else to use as rollers. Our makeshift crew worked quickly to get her out of the water and resting on the tires. Next, the Commune de Rangiroa backhoe, what Tahitians call the CASE, arrived. Teiva got our trailer and backed it down the beach. The backhoe driver expertly came through the coconut forest and down the beach. He slowly lifted *Vahine Iti* up in a sling and settled her gently back on her trailer. Teiva drove out through the coconut forest pulling a battered and bruised *Vahine Iti*. He had her back in our carport in a few minutes. Everyone was gone by noon. Scooter and I stood there staring at her, soggy and bashed. We were in shock.

That afternoon we got busy. We started by taking every single item out of *Vahine Iti*. Everything was totally soaked, even things that were secured in supposedly watertight containers. We laid everything out in the carport to dry. That perfect paint job Scooter had spent so much time on the week before was a wreck. Several holes, mostly on the sides, littered the formerly perfectly smooth hull. She sat there. We walked around her, stared, assessed the damage, and wondered out loud, "Can she be saved?" We weren't sure at that point. The sun set that evening on a beat-down captain and his downtrodden deckhand.

It turned out that we were in luck. We found out that Christopher, a longtime fishing pal of Scooter's, was not only an excellent fisherman but also an experienced fiberglasser.

He was (again, very luckily) in port in between fishing trips. Everyone we knew agreed that Christopher was the guy to help us. Another stroke of luck was that a tiny hardware store had just opened on the atoll. It was freshly stocked and had all the supplies Christopher would need for the repair. That, alone, was a miracle. After about ten days of drying out in our carport, Teiva and Scooter drove *Vahine Iti* over to Christopher's. She was there for about two weeks. During that time, Scooter would go over if Christopher needed a hand with hoisting, repositioning, or if he needed more supplies delivered from the hardware store. After Christopher was done with the repair, Scooter repainted the bottom.

We were totally amazed at the outcome. When Christopher brought her back, and after she was backed into our carport once again, we cracked open some Hinanos and fondly christened him "Dr. Christopher." His work was impeccable. Like a highly skilled surgeon, he had put her back together and made her beautiful and seaworthy once again. He will forever be one of our Rangiroa heroes.

Almost losing *Vahine Iti* made us realize just how much we had grown to enjoy our time with her. She had been out of the water for almost a month. While she was getting repaired, we bumbled around, a bit aimless, a bit depressed, and a bit sad. As soon as she was back in the water, we sprung back into our happy groove. These days if it's a good day for fishing or exploring the atoll, you can believe that we don't waste it.

— *POSTSCRIPT* —

We know the CASE driver, Rangi. He's Moana's brother-in-law. As he left that day, driving off in his backhoe, I tried to pay him. Teiva said, "No, you have to pay at the city hall after they make your bill." So, we waited a week or so, then went to pay. I took a big wad of francs thinking the worst. The bill totaled the equivalent of twenty-five US dollars.

After that perfect storm, we decided to leave Vahine Iti *in the* hoa *all the time. It's just a short walk down the road, and it's easier for Scooter to launch her from there.*

THE COCONUT MUFFLER

I just googled the term "MacGyver." Wikipedia's definition, in part, goes like this: "When one 'MacGyvers' a solution to a problem, one finds a simple yet elegant solution using existing resources." Reading on, the entry notes that "MacGyver uses a lot of duct tape, paper clips, chewing gum, a Swiss Army knife and shoelaces." MacGyver would have been right at home on a coral atoll.

In recent years, it's become slightly easier to find what you need in Rangiroa. Now there is a small hardware store that has some do-it-yourself supplies. The one and only gas station also has an array of fix-it items. While we use both stores, we mostly do what we have done for years: rely on our own know-how; a bit of creativity; some basic tools; and, like MacGyver, "chewing gum, paper clips, and duct tape."

Scooter has brought down an amazing assortment of tools.

You name it, he's got it. He's also brought a lot of basic hardware: nuts, bolts, screws, nails, etc. We have a whole section in our ACE Hardware cabinet dedicated to "things that hold things together." On that shelf, you will find a staple gun and staples, zip ties of every size and color, superglue, Elmer's glue, duct tape, a hot glue gun and glue sticks, rubber bands, a grommet kit, strings and smaller ropes, bungee cords of varying sizes, clamps and clips, hose clamps, hooks, hangers, and on and on. These are the items we use almost every day to do repairs, create things to make life easier or more visually pleasing, and to solve any boat, bike, or household breakdowns.

There are too many examples of our MacGyverisms to mention. It's just our way of life here. Creative thinking is the key to dealing with those little glitches that seem to pop up randomly and regularly. In Kona, a quick trip to Lowe's solves just about anything. Here, it takes some thought—maybe a walk around the yard past Moana's junk pile; a hike up the stairs to Scooter's Chinese Store; a stop at the ACE shelf where the "things that hold things together" live; and then, finally, taking a seat at our picnic table to fabricate what we need. Some creations are successful, and some fail. When they succeed, we pat ourselves on the back. When they fail, we start all over again with a new plan.

I will mention our favorite MacGyverism. It occurred long ago when we stayed with Manarii and his father, Petero. They rented us a sweet little bungalow down by sleepy Ohotu Village. It was a long trek to the main village of Avatoru, so we decided to rent a moped for the month. It was a cheap, old moped, but it got us everywhere we needed to go. The only issue was that it had no muffler. It would scream an ungodly sound as we rode down the road. Scooter, MacGyver reincarnated, looked around for some way to muffle that ear-shattering sound. He found a hollowed-out coconut, most likely eaten by rats. He stuck it in where the muffler should have been, secured it with some random wire, and voilà. Yes, the coconut got a bit warm and smoldered a little, but it worked. To us, this became the gold standard of all MacGyverisms as defined above by Wikipedia: a simple, elegant solution created using available materials.

One afternoon, Scarlett stopped by for a friendly game of Rummikub and a glass of wine. While playing, I told her about this current chapter. She's lived here for almost thirty years, so I figured that I'd have to explain to her who MacGyver was and what the term meant. "Have you ever heard of MacGyver?" I asked. I was totally shocked when she replied, "Oh yes! He's a national hero here!" Really? I had no idea that Tahitians knew anything about MacGyver. She went on to tell me that this place is referred to as the Land of MacGyver. I couldn't agree more with the sentiment.

SURFING RANGIROA

I wish this book was filled with vivid descriptions of my surfing exploits in Rangiroa. I would describe cutting back and forth on glassy, turquoise-blue waves. I'd take turns with the local crew in the unspoken rotation that naturally evolves when friends surf together. I would ride waves all morning until I'd be forced to call it quits from sheer exhaustion. I'd say my goodbyes to the gang and paddle back to *Vahine Iti,* anchored in the shallows. Scooter would be waiting in the shade of the Bimini top with a dry towel and a flask of ice-cold water. We'd pull the anchor and motor back through Avatoru Pass, then turn left and continue down the glassy lagoon to our house. We'd be silent, both of us thinking the same thing: this is about as good as it gets. Unfortunately, this dream sequence has never happened, and it never will. After years of scheming, thinking, planning, and trying, I have finally had to accept the fact that I'll never surf here on the atoll.

All my Kona surf buddies ask me about surfing in

Rangiroa. When I tell them there is surf, but that I don't surf it, everyone is shocked. My whole life revolves around surfing. It's been like that for close to forty years. It's hard to keep me out of the lineup. I guess you could say it's an addiction. I'm humbled and a bit amazed that I'm still able to surf at my age. My mantra is: Never Stop. Not surfing in Rangiroa is a hard pill for me to swallow; it goes against every fiber of my being, my mantra, and my daily routine.

Rangiroa has three breaks. The main break is in the Avatoru Pass. Scooter and I go out in *Vahine Iti* and watch the waves and surfers from the safety of the shoulder. We sit there as I analyze every wave and each ride. I watch the rotation of the surfers and see who is doing what. Many times, over the years, I think that I could and should ride that wave. But I know better.

The wave is just too steep, too hollow, and too fast for me. It's suited for the speed and maneuverability of a short board and requires the strength, stamina, and flexibility of a *taure'are'a* (teenager). On top of that, the wave breaks in very shallow water with sharp coral heads just below the surface. I've seen kids leave the beach with bleeding backs that look like freshly ground hamburger. Need one more reason why I'm not interested in this break? The passes of Rangiroa are known worldwide as the habitat of extra-large tiger sharks. People make long pilgrimages here just to dive with these apex predators. During the breeding season, the passes are teeming with tigers and, at times, hammerheads. Did I mention it's also the home of the gray reef shark? It's one of the most aggressive sharks out there, and it is to be avoided at all costs.

There was a time when I thought I might try to ride the inside shoulder of this wave. I would have needed a longboard, something about nine feet long. There is only one longboard I know of on the atoll. It belongs to Teiva. He traded fresh fruit for it with a traveling surfer cruising Tahiti by sailboat. That board hangs up in the rafters over Teiva's lanai. One day, I asked him if he would consider selling it to me. He rarely says no to anything, but this time his answer was definite. He told me that the board had sentimental value and that it wasn't for sale. I understand that completely, having a few special boards of my own. I never asked him again. After that avenue closed, I considered bringing a board; however, the length of a longboard exceeds the size limit for Air Tahiti's domestic flights. Then I thought, why not buy and bring a bisect board (a board that breaks in two for travel)? It would be under the size limit, and I'd finally have a longboard here for surfing the inside shoulder in Avatoru Pass. A friend in Kona had one. He offered to sell it to me. I went over to his place and checked it out. I brought the board home and practiced putting it together several times in our garage. In the end, I decided against the bisect. It was too complicated and too heavy to lug down, considering the massive quantities of luggage we already haul.

So, after all is said and done, it looks like I'll never surf in Rangiroa. Time is marching on, and my window has basically closed. But I can still dream. I'll always go and look at the waves and watch the surf from the safety of our boat. It's just part of my routine as a surfer. It really kills me that I'm not capable enough, don't have the equipment I need, and—most of all—that I am not brave enough for this wave right here in our backyard. Scooter and I talked about this. He told me to trust my instincts, and I do.

The break in Avatoru is well-known to Tahitian surfers. It's a right, and right breaks in French Polynesia are a bit rare. The waves break on north swells and can get sizable. Many surfers come here specifically for these waves. In recent years, this spot has become known internationally. Every year the atoll plays host to the worldwide surf community when it runs the Air Tahiti Rangiroa Pro. It's an exciting weeklong event, especially if the waves are big.

One day, I saw a beautiful stand-up paddleboard (SUP) under William's *fare pote'e* next door. It looked like it had never been used. I asked him about it. He told me he had shipped it over from Pape'ete for his kids to play on when they visited him from Mo'orea. Was it for sale by any chance? He lit up. Yes! We struck a deal, and I carried the SUP and its companion, the long SUP paddle, past the palm frond fence and into our yard.

I've never gotten into canoe paddling, SUP surfing, or SUP long-distance paddling. I've always preferred basic longboarding on breaking waves and prone paddling on my surfboard on totally flat days. I wasn't even sure if I was going to like my new water toy, let alone figure out how to paddle it efficiently. Scarlett hooked me up with the top female SUP paddler on the atoll. Mahana lives close by. She agreed to give me a bit of a rundown on SUPs. I rode over on my bike, carrying my long SUP paddle in one hand. We hit it off right away, both of us being watergirls. We took her two racing SUPs out in the lagoon just in front of her house. They were streamlined and tippy, but I have good balance and arm strength, so I did OK. As usual, the language barrier got in the way. I found that my Tahitian vocabulary didn't include the technical terms she used. With gestures and demonstrations, she gave me tips and pointers. After that, I was on my own.

Surprisingly, I have really enjoyed paddling my SUP. It requires a glassy day, which is rare. I always paddle into the wind and current so that when I turn around, the home stretch is easier. Gliding over coral heads in crystal-clear water is mesmerizing. I'm transfixed by the activity of hundreds of colorful fish below. Blacktip sharks glide by, giant manta rays fly along the edge of the turquoise water where it changes to cobalt blue, eagle rays cruise in the shallows, and barracuda fiercely hug coral heads and look out baring big, ugly teeth. There's a resident nurse shark I've seen several times. They are such odd creatures not only in looks, with their flat, broad heads and pointed tails, but also in behavior. Sometimes I dive in the water just to cool off and take a break from paddling. I got to know an incredibly beautiful and sassy Brazilian woman who was living solo on a trimaran anchored along my route. I'd stop and chat while still standing on my SUP next to her boat. We'd have a few laughs together, and then I'd be on my way again. Paddling a SUP does not give me that rush of riding waves, but it's a pretty good substitute.

There are only a few things I miss while we are in Rangiroa: good avocados and surfing being two on that short list. Just before we pack up and leave, we email our house sitter and ask her to kindly stock up on some avocados for us. When we arrive in Kona, there's no unpacking to do. All four suitcases come back totally empty. That leaves me with an open agenda to go catch some early morning glass at my favorite spot.

BABYSITTER NO LONGER REQUIRED

People here have been so good to us. Close friends have helped us since day one. Complete strangers have also helped us. Help has come our way at random times and in random ways. Help has appeared in many forms and has been in gestures both large and small. The simple kindness of so many people has been humbling. We accept what is offered, and we are thankful beyond words. We always make it a point of honor to repay kindness in one way or another. Although the help is welcome, as time moves on, we have been working our way toward self-sufficiency. As with everything here, it has been a slow and steady journey.

We have decided that the key to our self-sufficiency is our access to transportation. Having transportation is something taken for granted in our other life: hop in the car, go where you want, see who you need to see, get to an appointment, load up supplies and groceries, and return home carrying everything in the back seat. It's just so easy. Transportation on Rangiroa, on the other hand, has been a tremendous stumbling block.

At first, we had one-speed pedal bikes. We left some money at the end of one trip, and, in our absence, Scarlett bought them for us when a shipment of bikes arrived by cargo ship. She and Rich put them under their house and covered them with a tarp. There was one lime-green bike and one wine-colored bike waiting for us upon our return. It was thrilling to finally have our own bikes. Over the years, we have always rented bikes. As with most rental equipment, the condition of the bikes was usually questionable, and the cost was outrageous. With our own bikes, we could oversee their routine maintenance and make small improvements, like adding a second basket, a better kickstand, softer seats, and more comfortable handlebar grips.

Riding bikes here should be easy. The atoll is flat. Truthfully, riding bikes in Rangiroa can be extremely hard and very dangerous. There is usually a strong headwind that, at times, can completely stop the forward motion of a bike. The poor condition of the road is another factor. The "road," if you could call it that, is basically one big pothole after another for the six miles between Avatoru and Ohotu Villages. To be fair, there are a few decent stretches. Despite the Commune de Rangiroa's best efforts, this is not a place to enjoy a leisurely bike ride. The road is narrow, so when two cars meet, both pull off a bit to their respective sides to pass each other and avoid a head-on crash. If you're on a bike where the two cars meet, get out of the way. Getting out of the way involves riding off the high, jagged edge of asphalt and then plowing through either soft sand or bumpy coral on the shoulder. All of this is not easy to negotiate while getting away from the opposing cars in a duel. Now, add to all that excitement the weight of the groceries you are hauling in two baskets and in your overstuffed backpack, and you will get the whole, wobbly picture. In a nutshell, bike riding is more like an endurance event at a motocross rally.

When we had bicycles as our only form of transportation, we needed help from others. We needed a ride to the *magasin* to buy and bring home *bonbonnes* (five-gallon drinking water bottles). We needed a ride to the gas station to buy *gaz* (propane tanks) and five-gallon cans of *essence* (gasoline for *Vahine Iti*). We could handle the groceries on our own, but these heavier items were impossible to transport on a bicycle. Scooter even tried to MacGyver a little trailer for his bike to haul big items, with little success.

After a while, we figured out that we could take *Vahine Iti* to the small marina in Avatoru to at least get the *essence* by ourselves. We discovered a guy who pumped gasoline out of a shipping container on the dock on weekday mornings between six and nine. It wasn't easy, but it felt good not to have to rely on others for just this one thing. While tied up in the village, we could also pick up groceries at the *magasin* close to the marina. We would walk them back to the boat, load up, head home down the lagoon in our boat, and off-load on our beach.

The next step for us was to buy a motor scooter. While in

Kona, Scooter had been watching the online ads on the Tahiti Infos website. After about a month, he spotted what he'd been looking for: a vintage Vespa. Just a few days before we came back down, we arranged to meet the owners of the Vespa in Pape'ete at the airport in between our arrival from Hawaii and our departure to Rangiroa. After a cash deal, the owners gave us all the signed paperwork, and then they promised to deliver the Vespa to the *Dory*—the regular interisland cargo ship that comes from Pape'ete once each week with fresh food and supplies—for shipping. We caught our flight to Rangiroa and prayed that they were honest folk and didn't just take the cash and keep the Vespa.

Within a week, the Vespa arrived in Rangiroa. We thought, "Wow, we finally have our own transportation." All we needed was insurance. As with buying *Vahine Iti*, there was a glitch—a big glitch. We could not get insurance. Everyone tried to help us. To get insurance, you need a French Polynesian driver's license. To get that license, you must take a written test. That test is, of course, in French. We thought we could take the test using our translation app on our phone, or see if the *gendarme* would allow Scarlett to come as our translator. While trying to solve this problem, we finally found out that even if we got a Polynesian driver's license, we could not be insured anyway. We were considered too old to be able to handle a motor scooter safely. We now had a viable mode of transportation that we couldn't legally use. While a lot of people here drive without insurance, as guests, we do not want any problems with the *gendarme*. We do use the Vespa, but sparingly, and never on a Friday afternoon when a checkpoint is usually set up by the airport.

The final step to gaining self-sufficiency was so easy. It was odd that it took us so long to figure it out. The electric bike cost about eight hundred US dollars. Besides *Vahine Iti*, it was the best investment we've made so far. Scooter added a big basket to the back. He's able to go everywhere he needs on a single charge. He can carry an oversized *gaz* bottle if he is careful. I can ride on the back if we need to go somewhere together. At this point, no insurance is required for electric bikes in Tahiti. Life is looking up.

Teiva still stops in and picks up Scooter to go to the gas station. Why? It's a guy thing, I guess. They just like hanging out together. They leave laughing and come home laughing. Scarlett and I will go shopping together sometimes just because we like to be together, too. Why not?

A while back, we were all packed up and ready to leave after three months on the atoll. Teiva and Meho stopped in to say goodbye. We always have fun with those two, and we've done our fair share of laughing together. Teiva really got us laughing harder than usual when his parting words were, "I didn't even have to babysit you guys this time." We had finally reached the point of self-sufficiency, and, yes, we no longer required a babysitter.

— POSTSCRIPT —

Scooter, at age seventy-five, rides an 850-pound Harley-Davidson Road King on Kona roads. Funny, he's considered too old to be insured to ride the Vespa.

That Vespa was pretty much a mess when she arrived on the cargo ship. Scooter, a lifelong car guy, has, little by little, restored her to perfection. He even gave her a "Rangiroa paint job" using cans of spray paint to spray one Vespa piece at a time in a jerry-rigged spray booth out in the coconut forest.

I witnessed how the concrete portions of the road are laid in Rangiroa. Believe it or not, the wet concrete is poured out within wooden frames set up on both sides of the road. Two workers on opposite sides of the road take a long, heavy metal pipe and hand-roll the concrete out as a team. This is done a few feet at a time. There's very little in the way of equipment, just the cement mixer. Now I know why it takes forever to complete road improvements.

I'm still riding the lime-green one-speed bike. It's a bit rusty now, but it's still running smoothly, and it gets me where I need to go.

SHARKS

Seeing a shark is always exciting. They are fascinating and intriguing animals. Many people abhor them. Many people worship them. I guess I fall somewhere in the middle. I have a healthy respect for sharks, and usually, I'm not afraid when I see one. Usually.

This lagoon is filled with sharks, mostly blacktips. There are so many sharks that we have become desensitized to them. They are like ants—they're everywhere. We sit at the breakfast table, eating fruit and toast, and watch the silent fins glide past in the totally glassy water. While having a light lunch of crackers and cheese, we see more fins go by, then watch as they swerve over the coral head just to the left. Cocktail hour finds us enjoying rum and mango juice. As we quietly talk, we spot more fins in the darkening turquoise water. We usually yell, "*Ma'o!*" (shark) when we see one and point to its location. All day, every day, they are there. That's just how it is here.

I'm in the lagoon every day, swimming. Funnily enough, I usually don't see any sharks when I'm out there. They are there, though. I don't go out too far, but it really doesn't matter. They are close to shore, out far by our buoy, and everywhere in between.

One morning, Scooter had a blacktip shark turn around to take a second and then a third pass at him while he was simply putting on his fins at the edge of the lagoon. He was about to swim out to do a routine mooring check. That third pass had him jump up and back on the shore, swim fins and mask flying. It was a bit "off" for the usual blacktip behavior. That got our attention. I duct-taped a knife to a long metal pole, and then we swam out together, side by side. From that point on, we made it our standard operating procedure to go out to the mooring as a team. He'd do the inspection and any necessary chain adjusting, and I'd keep watch with my long knife-tipped pole. We brought down Sharkbanz on the next trip after that little encounter. Teiva just laughs at these contraptions, but we strap them on our ankles when we tag team out to the mooring.

In the very early mornings when I'm on the road for my run, I see all kinds of interesting wildlife. One March, just as the first light was showing, I stopped to watch blacktips circling and doing figure eights in the *hoa* by Mrs. Tetuanui's house. Looking straight down from the bridge, a few feet above the water makes for excellent viewing. There may have been two hundred sharks. It was hard to tell because they were all constantly moving at different depths, and swimming in silent patterns only they understood. There would be an occasional outburst accompanied by a violent splash, then a fast bite toward another shark. It was eerie. Tahi showed up and watched, too. After watching the show for a while, I turned and took off on my run. By the time I returned, all the sharks were gone. I saw them there morning after morning in the dawning light. On our most recent trip, we were here in March again. I wondered if I'd be lucky enough to be treated to that predawn shark show. Was it seasonal? I didn't know. I looked every morning and only saw a few sharks circling and doing their figure eights. I described what I saw to the local hammerhead shark expert. He had never seen that behavior before and didn't know what it was all about. I have come to the conclusion that this is blacktip mating behavior.

Long ago we went with Teiva and Meho in their boat outside; that's outside the atoll in the open ocean, known here as *e tua*. When we jumped on board that morning, Scooter and I didn't know where we were going or what we were going to do, but we knew it would be some sort of adventure. We ended up way around the corner just outside the area known as Lagon Bleu. Teiva pulled his boat close to the reef where the waves were breaking and set the anchor. I always told myself that I'd never, ever in a million years get in the ocean outside the atoll. I knew too much already about sharks. Teiva was going to free dive. He told us that while he was down, we were to watch for the gray reef shark. "That's the bad one," he said. "Don't worry about the other ones." While we weren't exactly sure what we were looking for, we knew we could stand guard. As soon as we jumped in, Teiva was gone. Immediately sharks started charging us, making us feel like bait. They came from every direction and every depth. Which one were we supposed to look out for? They all looked the same to me. They would swim directly toward us and then do a last-minute U-turn.

I lasted all of one minute. It was a pretty poor showing for a seasoned watergirl. I was up the ladder and back in the boat, shaking from that up-close and personal experience. Scooter, taking his guard duty seriously, stayed put. In the boat, Meho was trying to prepare lunch. I was attempting to help her, but the swirling sharks hitting the boat had us both on edge. My hat is off to Scooter, who remained true to his friend and survived that little escapade. Afterward, the four of us ate lunch, bobbing up and down in the boat surrounded by all the sharks. That was the first, last, and only time I dove into the open ocean in the Tuamotus.

One sparkling atoll morning I was working in the yard, raking sand as usual. I'd had enough for the day. Scooter and I said in unison, "Guess it's lunchtime." We were both hungry. As we were walking up the steps to the lanai, we spotted something floating in the lagoon. It was inflated, like a ball, and light gray in color. It was drifting our way with the prevailing wind and current. It was just out where the turquoise meets cobalt blue. "What is that?" we asked each other at exactly the same time. We took turns looking through the binoculars. It looked like the carcass of a baby dolphin. We figured it must have come through the *hoa* by Mrs. Tetuanui's. Just then a big, ugly form swirled, rose out of the water, opened its jaws, and attacked that bloated body. We froze and watched the carnage. The attack seemed to be never-ending. I'd never seen anything like it. Scooter has seen it all with a lifetime of fishing. Not me. We watched as the tiger shark came back, over and over and over again, from every angle and every direction, until the bloated body was completely devoured. Then it fell silent and completely still. I just stood there, my binoculars limp at my side. I was sickened and in shock. It was, in one word, gruesome. I'll never forget it. We returned to the idea of having some lunch. Even though I had been hungry just minutes before, I had completely lost my appetite. A stiff rum drink would have been more agreeable.

We have a resident nurse shark that cruises along this stretch of the lagoon. It's an odd color, something reminiscent of Army green. It's large, possibly nine feet long. It swims along the bottom, rooting up coral while searching for crustaceans to eat. It looks like most other species of shark, with one exception: its tail is pointed. By all accounts, this type of shark is not dangerous. We believe this particular shark is the same one that swims by Teiva and Meho's house about a half-mile away. They warned us not to feed it. If fed, it becomes a pest and just hangs out, waiting for the next meal. This shark's territory is between Moana's Village and the Kia Ora Hotel. Back and forth, it swims all day and all night long. We are always on the lookout for this very odd creature. When it shows up, we yell "nurse shark" and run to the edge of the lagoon to observe its behavior.

People from all over the world come to Rangiroa to dive. Many specifically come to interact with sharks. It's all the rage right now to commune with large tigers in the passes. When a tiger is spotted, divers hold steady on the floor of the lagoon. As the shark approaches, the diver faces it squarely and holds out his hand in a STOP gesture. Slowly, the immense shark comes forward, bumps that outstretched hand with its nose, then gently turns and swims away. That is something that would totally freak me out. I am brave, but not that brave.

GONE FISHING

It was a real stroke of luck to cross paths (literally) with Scooter. I was on the Big Island of Hawaii for only a week. A ridiculous love affair with a Tahitian had gone upside down, and instead of a week in Bora Bora, I was in Kona, trying to forget that *tane*. I wanted nothing more to do with men. All I wanted to do was surf, see friends, and run along Ali'i Drive in the early mornings.

On Wednesday of that week, I ended up at the ugliest, smelliest place around: the haul-out ramp at Honokohau Harbor dry dock. There I was with time on my hands while my friend's catamaran was getting hauled out. Since I wanted nothing more to do with men, I shocked myself with a head jerk and a heart flip when a cute guy walked past me right next to an overflowing industrial dumpster. That was my first sighting of the man who is still by my side: Captain Scott M. Fuller/Big Game Fisherman (as stated on his business card).

By Sunday evening, we were engaged. Just before I boarded my flight back to California, he promised he would learn to surf, and I promised I would learn to fish. He learned how to surf, and he got pretty good, real fast. I never followed through on my part of the deal. Sure, I'd go out with him on the big, fancy charter boats, but I'd take my surfboard so that he could drop me off for a few waves while he went trolling down the line. Here I am, thirty-three years later, letting the world know that I have finally kept my promise: I am learning to fish.

When we first got *Vahine Iti,* we mainly used her to explore the atoll and pick up supplies. There were two rod holders on the boat, but Scooter said, "They're not in the right place." I didn't know much about rod holders, but even I could tell they were oddly placed and basically useless. So, onward we went for the first few years, just happily cruising about, enjoying the natural wonders of Rangiroa.

During this period of cruising, we began to work together as a boating team. He knew how to be a captain. I was learning to be a deckhand. He was my teacher. I've been on boats all my life, but this was different. It was very apparent that I needed a lot of training. I needed to learn to use the gaff (a long pole with a hook) and use it with accuracy. I needed to learn to tie off bumpers, quickly, if necessary. I needed to hook a cleat on a dock without missing. I needed to lower the motor and know exactly when to stop to avoid the coral heads below. I needed to remember to raise the ladder while underway and drill it into my head that dragging a ladder affects optimal boat performance. I needed to know how to gently start the engine so it does not overwork. Most importantly, I needed to learn how to handle the boat by myself in case something happened to Scooter out on the water.

We discovered we worked well together on a boat. Our routines improved and smoothed out over time, and our groove began to flow. We also discovered that the size of *Vahine Iti* was perfect for the two of us. We learned how to utilize the cramped space with consideration for each other and how to move with efficiency. It's a bit like a dance.

Preparing the boat to shove off is a two-person job. We slowly fell into the routine of doing our respective tasks, silently and effortlessly. We needed not only to prepare the boat, but we also had to close the house for the day and provision *Vahine Iti* with food and drinks. With practice and time, we were shoving off as smooth as butter.

Somehow, we came to the unspoken conclusion that we were done with just cruising. We were finally ready to go fishing. Maybe it was because we got better at handling our boat. Maybe it was because this lagoon inspired us. Maybe it was because we were just ready for a bit of a change. For whatever reason, we were ready.

On our last trip, we brought new rod holders to install, three fishing poles (one for Teiva), and a lot of tackle and gear. We were set to go. It was within a week that *Vahine Iti* was up on the reef with holes in her hull from the bashing she took during that perfect storm. After Christopher got her repaired, we relaunched her and didn't waste any time. We only had about a month left in our stay. We made a tentative foray into lagoon fishing, but time ran out on us, and we left the atoll wanting more.

Scooter has spent his entire adult life fishing for marlin, tuna, mahi-mahi, and ono. These are big game fish found in the open ocean. His main tactic is trolling with lures or live bait rigged up to four or five big rods and reels. He knows what signs to look for and has honed his instincts about where to fish. His biggest marlin was 968 pounds, and he was honored to win the Hawaiian International Billfish Tournament one year. He's a very humble man, and the only reason I mention this is to put our Rangiroa fishing endeavors into perspective. We are learning about lagoon fishing. It's a totally different game than what he's done and known for years out in the open ocean.

In this new game, he has met new challenges. He has created different lures after noting what the fish respond to. He can sit for an entire afternoon at the big picnic table and mix and match colors, feathers, beads, and setups on the tiny lures. He's trying different trolling speeds, and, after quite a bit of experimenting, he has settled on the speed that gets results. He's finding different routes along the lagoon, learning which coral heads to hug, which ones to circle, and which to avoid. It's a game of observation and modification.

I am learning right alongside him. We are both learning about the lagoon fish, their names in Tahitian, and if they are keepers that will go on the dinner table.

When we fish, I am the angler, and with that role comes another whole set of things to learn. While Scooter drives, he's focused on what's in front of him, looking for signs of fish and watching the coral heads. I'm facing backward, watching the poles and the trailing lures. As I watch the tips of the rods, I am focused on any sign of a bite. When we get a bite, I'm up on my feet and removing the rod from its holder. I get situated back on my stool and angle the fish to the boat. My technique is primitive because I'm still learning. I'm always excited no matter what I reel in. Scooter takes the leader (wire line next to the hook) as the fish arrives near the boat and removes the hook. Then we decide: is it a keeper, or should we toss it back so that it can grow bigger? These are small fish, but they can put up a good fight. I've caught a few pretty good ones so far, and now I'm totally hooked on fishing! It only took me thirty-three years to make this discovery.

— *POSTSCRIPT* —

Coincidentally, at the time we crossed paths by that smelly dumpster, Scooter was the president of the "He-Man Woman Haters Club" (title compliments of The Little Rascals*), having just been dumped by a girlfriend. Neither one of us was looking, and, well, you see what happened.*

While I was writing this chapter, Scooter was sitting across the big picnic table from me. He's been online ordering new lure skirts and a fishing harness for me.

WATER

When we began our five-year lease and moved into our shack in the sand, Moana and Tarona had already moved to Pape'ete. Esther, Moana's sister, met us that first day with the house key and gave us the nickel tour. She speaks very little English, and our French is totally fractured, so our induction ceremony was greatly lacking. We attained a bit of mutual understanding using gestures and speaking some Tahitian. She showed us the Cash Power box on the wall and explained how to use it. We'd never used such a system, but we would learn. She showed us the breaker box in the bathroom. That was easy. It's just like our breaker in Kona.

Then Esther showed us the two large catchment tanks in the side yard. We were very curious about how the water system worked. She demonstrated how to tell how much water is in the tanks: simply knock on the side of the big, black tank while going up and down, and listen for where the echo is different. Where the sound is different is where the water level is located. She demonstrated again. We watched and listened. I knocked a few times. I nodded to indicate that I heard a different sound at one specific spot, when, in reality, I did not.

The next stop on the tour was the water pump closet behind the house. There were two blue mechanisms that looked like they came straight out of a Dr. Seuss illustration. Those were the pumps. Rope was wrapped around pipes at various junctures. There were valves, switches, wires, and plugs. Several black, greasy oil spots littered the cement floor below the confusing mishmash of machinery. It looked like a bowl of blue spaghetti to me. Understanding the machinery was beyond my comprehension. When she closed the pump closet door, I was relieved. I struggle with processing visual chaos. I sure hoped that MacGyver Fuller had taken in what I could not.

Esther left, and we were on our own. Scarlett, our guardian angel, stopped by later to fill in the missing pieces of the puzzle. With her help, we got the Cash Power procedure under control. We also gained a better understanding of how a catchment system works. What none of us knew that day was that the intricacies of this particular water pump system were many. We would soon learn all about it—the hard way.

Everyone in Rangiroa uses catchment tanks. Every house has at least one tank in the yard. Every house has a pump system as a companion to the tanks. The rain falls, and it's naturally siphoned from the rain gutter on the roof down through large pipes leading to the top of the tanks. It falls into the tank and sits there until you need it at the tap. The pump kicks on with a high-pitched squeal every time the water is turned on. Hearing that pump go on and off takes a little getting used to.

Moana, born and raised in Rangiroa, went to extreme measures with our water system. Being an atoll boy, he knows firsthand about the importance of never running out of water. Our two aboveground tanks hold *pape ua*, beautiful, pristine rainwater. They are interconnected, meaning they rise and fall together as if they are one tank. Although initially we didn't know of its existence, there is also an underground cistern, a natural water shelf that Moana had lined with concrete. This holds the brackish water that flows in on very high tides or during big swells. That water is called *pape 'apo'o*. It's there as a backup if we ever go dry. *Pape ua* and *pape 'apo'o* each have a pump in the Seussian blue spaghetti closet.

Pumps don't live forever. Our pump for the *pape ua* had a meltdown one time. In Scooter's words, "It seized up." Pierre, the Barefoot Plumber, arrived with his sidekick, Poe. Thankfully, he had a new pump in stock. What luck. We thought they would be here for a few hours. As usual, it was the Lucy, Desi, Fred, and Ethel show. Pierre was working in the blue spaghetti closet on the pumps. Poe was running around grabbing and delivering tools to him. Scooter and I were trying to assist. As usual, I was using my Tahitian with Poe to relay thoughts on repair ideas between Pierre and

Scooter. It ended up being a full day of crazy madness. When they finally rolled out of our driveway, we were relieved that our pump was fixed and that it was also cocktail hour.

It took about two days for us to figure out that something was still not right with the water system. The water coming out of the tap was brown and smelled like rotten eggs. Esther came by. It was at this point that Esther explained the existence of that underground cistern that stores the *pape 'apo'o*. While Pierre had replaced our pump for the beautiful rainwater, he had neglected to turn it back on, leaving the smelly *pape 'apo'o* flowing. Esther knew exactly what happened. Pierre would need to be called again.

After a few days, Scooter was fed up with stinky showers while waiting for Pierre to appear. He took matters into his own hands. He got in that Dr. Seuss closet and, step by step, followed the lines and valves to figure out what was what. With determination, he untangled the mess and got our precious rainwater flowing once again. Unfortunately, Esther had already called Pierre to come back and switch out the pumps. We were unable to call him, so we left him a note. It said, THE WATER PUMP IS FIXED. We reasoned that when he showed up, the note would stop him from turning the good water pump off and the bad water pump back on. We went out that day, and when we came back, it appeared that the pumps had not been touched. The note was still taped to the water pump closet. We figured Pierre had never been able to come by, so we promptly forgot all about the Case of the Switching Water Pumps.

A few weeks later, we were at a *magasin* down in Ohotu Village. We ran into Terii, Teiva's son. While we were talking story with him out in the parking lot, Pierre drove up. He came right up to the three of us in a flurry. He asked Terii to ask us about that note. He had come by and seen it but hadn't known what it had said. We explained it all to Terii, and he relayed the story to Pierre. That's just how things go for us.

As our time here has passed, we've turned into atoll people if, for no other reason, we are obsessed with water. Water is the big, big topic on everyone's mind. We look for black clouds and call out to them, "Please, clouds, come this way." We talk about rain with everyone and compare the levels in our respective tanks. We walk out and tap the tanks after every rainstorm and try to calculate how much the level has risen. If no rain has arrived in a while, we tap, tap, tap and hope that some is on the way. We are always worrying and always thinking about water.

— *POSTSCRIPT* —

I have never figured out how the water tank tapping system works. Scooter says that it's easy. So, I just rely on him for the good news or the bad news about our water level.

Since that incident, we have gotten better at using our handheld translator. In retrospect, we should have used it to write the note to Pierre in French.

MAGIC TIME

It is Wednesday. We're getting things pulled together to leave on Saturday. As usual, a big, gray cloud is parked over me, and I've been tearing up all day at odd moments. We have built a paradise here. I'm never ready to leave. It happens every time. For some reason, I'm really dragging my feet more than usual. Life in Hawaii isn't bad. I'll go surf the south swells at my spot for three months, and Scooter will do some summer tournament fishing. Nevertheless, I always miss this atoll life.

Thinking Scooter felt the same way, I was shocked when he gritted his teeth this morning just before breakfast and said, "I can't wait to get out of here!" He's got some god-awful rash on his leg, and it's driving him crazy. This rash only happens in Rangiroa. We've tried everything to quell its severe itch. Nothing has worked. After a hot compress offered some much-needed relief, he was in a greatly improved frame of mind. I asked him about his "getting out of here" comment. He reneged and said it was just the rash talking.

To be fair, about six months ago, I'd had it, too. The word used here is *fiu*, fed up. After three and a half years with great neighbors at Moana's Village, the newly arrived, inconsiderate neighbors were finally getting to me. That's when I threw up my hands and said, "Let's get out of here." I was ready to pack up and leave for good. Scooter reined me back in the next day. Together we decided that we're not quitters. We have too much invested here to just walk away; besides, this place is magical. After his pep talk, we were back on track.

It's been a roller-coaster ride. I won't lie. There have been good days and bad days. There have been many challenges requiring us to adapt, modify, and adjust our way of thinking and our way of life. On the plus side, we have both enjoyed living in a beautiful place with exceptionally nice people in a culture that inspires us. The rewards far outweigh the *fiu* times. If I had to pick the biggest and best reward, it would be that Scooter and I are on this adventure together. We really are yin and yang, and that combination seems to work for us as we navigate this entirely different life experience.

The previous Sunday night, I had come down with a bug. Monday found me rolling about in stomach pain combined with a high fever. On Tuesday, thinking I had greatly improved, we decided to go fishing. Not ten minutes after we set out, I got those stomach spasms again. We had to turn around. I just couldn't bounce around in a boat quite yet. He dropped me off on our beach and promptly went back out and caught two nice fish. So, that brings us back to today, Wednesday.

After a rocky start dealing with the leg rash, we decided to try going out in the boat again, hoping that my stomach would cooperate. *Vahine Iti* was getting hauled out in the afternoon. It was our last chance. We hopped aboard and did the pass-to-pass cruise, going slowly and taking everything in. It would be our last ride in our little boat for a while. We weren't talking much, just a few words here and there. We were both simply looking and soaking in everything at a place we've been lucky enough to call home.

Scooter picked the perfect playlist for us. There was a lot of jazz, some Van Morrison, and a few other favorite artists. One Van song was one I'd never heard before, "Magic Time." For some reason, I tuned everything else out and focused on the lyrics. It was just me and Van for a few minutes there in the turquoise-blue water. In the song, he reminisces about returning to his magic days in a special place with a special love. Every word in the song resonated with me. We've all had those magic times. Most of the time we're not even aware that those days are magic when they are happening. It's usually only later, with hindsight, that we come to that realization.

I know one thing for certain: these days, right here, right now, are my magic times. When I'm sitting in a wheelchair unable to do much of anything at the end of life, I will remember this adventure on a coral atoll that I shared with my incredible husband, and wonder how we pulled it off.

— POSTSCRIPT —

There is only one thing that would make this adventure any better. I'd give anything to have Mom and Dad sitting on our lanai under the thatch with us. We'd listen to the good old Tahitian music, drink a sip of rum, and watch the parade of canoes and boats pass by out front. They would have gotten a real kick out of it. They were responsible for my lifelong love affair with Tahiti. I think of them (and thank them) every day, especially when we're right here under the thatch.

TAHITIAN RADIO

There's really no need for us to listen to Tahitian radio. But we do. We've downloaded hundreds of songs on our iPads, everything from boot-stomping country western to reggae. Nevertheless, we find ourselves tuning into the radio.

Tahitian radio is a bit like fingernails on a chalkboard to us. But we still listen. We can take it only so long, then one of us cracks and turns the radio off in a haze of crazed insanity. It stays off for a while, and then we agree to give it another chance. Maybe it's gotten better, we think, so we turn it back on. We are on this hamster wheel with Tahitian radio, but it never changes, and it never gets any better.

There is only one station out here in the Tuamotus. It's broadcast from Tahiti. Most of the time it's talk radio. The host, Pablo, takes calls from everyone. He listens patiently as the caller drones on ceaselessly about a problem, a current political or social issue, or just wants to publicly proclaim unwavering love to his *vahine*. Then a bell dings, and time is up. Callers generally ignore the time limit. Pablo tries to rein them in, with no luck whatsoever.

Very rarely is any music played. When it is, we never know what we'll get. Just now we turned on the radio, and "Islands in the Stream," sung by Dolly Parton and Kenny Rogers, was playing. The music can swing from a German polka to a Mexican serenade and then on to an Elvis classic when, and if, three songs are ever played in a row. It's entertaining for us to guess what will be on when we flip the switch.

Besides a lot of talk and very little music, there's the news. The news is in French and then a bit later in Tahitian, so it goes on for twice as long. Many times, Tahitian and French are mixed, making for a third hybrid language and even more news time. Then there are the commercials. One jingle has been played incessantly for years. Scarlett absolutely, positively cannot listen to it one more time. She told us she turns the radio off as soon as it starts to play.

There is one saving grace on the Tahitian radio. On Saturdays and Sundays, they play Tahitian and Hawaiian music. The good kind. Many of the old Tahitian songs take me back to my childhood and right into the house where I grew up. Mom and Dad had their Tahitian LPs spinning endlessly on the hi-fi with all of us kids swinging our hips to the beat of the *to'ere* drums. I can somehow sing every word of the oldies. It's some deep, deep memory from sixty years ago, and it all comes back, magically, as soon as an oldie starts to play. It amazes me that something like that can stay inside your brain and pop out at a random moment so many years later.

Given this chaotic radio hodgepodge, why do we even listen? The real reason I tune in is to hear the Tahitian language. Even though it's spoken so quickly on the radio, just hearing words, phrases, and sometimes even complete sentences that I understand bolsters my confidence in learning the language. Usually, I can get the gist of what is being said, although my brain is always a few seconds behind with my internalized translation. Scooter has refused to study Tahitian. Why should he? He's got me. It's cool when he understands some words that he hears on the radio, too. He knows a lot more Tahitian than he fesses up to.

Both of us listen to the weather report. The wind directions are given; these directional terms are terms we are both learning. We have our custom-made Tahitian wind compass pillow for a handy reference if needed.

Lastly, I listen because it also helps with my French. My passion is Tahitian, but I'm learning French by default. "*Écoute, écoute*," (listen, listen) were the words I can still vividly hear my high school French teacher blare into my headphones in the language lab way back when. Never imagining where my life would lead, I paid scant attention in French class. If only I had listened better.

— POSTSCRIPT —

Since our little radio has given us a huge amount of listening frustration, I am happy to report that we have found a valid use for it: as an anti-theft device. When we go fishing for the day, if we leave the house open, we leave the radio on. That way, it sounds like someone is home.

XXXL STORM OF THE CENTURY

Teiva had warned me about spending so much time sifting the sand on our beach. He reminded me of what I already instinctively knew: one big storm, and my perfectly groomed beach would be destroyed. Even worse, all that beautiful, golden sand could be transported inside our kitchen. He's been on the atoll for his entire life, and he's seen it happen before.

I took Teiva's advice and backed off my crazy sand-sifting madness. By then the sand was soft, deep, and flawless, so I guess you could say I'd completed the project. Seeking more local wisdom, I asked our landlord, Moana, how high the lagoon water had ever come. He pointed to the corner of our lanai and said, "Only one night the water came up to here." At the time Moana had relayed this information to me, our house was already ten years old. I figured that only once in ten years was pretty good odds. The likelihood of that happening again was slim. Or so I thought.

One of the best things about Hawaiian TV news coverage is the excellent weather reporting. I make it a point to watch the weather every evening. A whole segment is devoted to the surf report. Though I watch carefully, I usually take the report with a grain of salt. It seems like the hype of an incoming swell far exceeds what actually shows up. In addition to the TV surf forecast, I use the tried and true method of simply looking out my window with my own two eyes. I look to Kaiwi Point to see which direction the waves are hitting: south in the summer, north in the winter. I look to see how big the white water is and how frequently waves smack the lava point. I watch Kaiwi morning, noon, and evening all year round. Seeing what's going on out there tells me where and when to surf. Some days I can see that the waves are just too big for me. That's when I get out the mop and plan a day of cleaning the lanais. I did pay extra close attention in mid-July when the bold, red letters splayed across the TV screen said, "XXXL SOUTH SWELL." Seeing that warning took me right back to our little shack in the sand we'd left one month prior. The shack faces directly south, and we have seen large swells roll across the immense lagoon and flood our shoreline. The water level rises a few feet, and, after a few days, everything returns to normal. The highest watermarks I'd seen so far never got too close to my groomed sand. I still wasn't too worried until I saw the words the next evening, again in bold red, "SOUTH XXXL SWELL OF THE CENTURY." That got my full attention.

At that point, I followed the tracking of this exceptional swell with hypervigilance. I suddenly became more worried about our shack in the sand, let alone the beach. Our house is approximately forty feet from the edge of the lagoon. There is a mildly sloping rise to the lanai, placing the house at, possibly, two feet above sea level. There is one small step up to the lanai. That step is a mere eight inches. Flooding was a huge possibility. Destroying the house, another.

As predicted, the swell arrived in French Polynesia and was deemed Code Red, meaning no person could enter the ocean for any reason. Those doing so risked arrest by the *gendarmes*. In an island nation populated with strong, passionate watermen and waterwomen, keeping people out of the ocean is usually impossible. This swell was different. People stayed on shore, watching the carnage out at sea and as the incredibly powerful surges invaded the land.

I emailed Teiva and Meho; our next-door neighbor, William; and Waiapa and Teura, other friends nearby. Rich and Scarlett, who normally watch over our place, were in Wyoming on vacation. I asked everyone there to keep an eye on our place. It really didn't matter who I contacted; nothing, absolutely nothing, can be done when it comes to Mother Nature's relentless advance. Everyone was bracing for the worst-case scenario.

The first surge didn't seem too bad. Teiva and Meho went over to our place and took a few photos of the rising water.

As I looked at their pictures on my iPad, I felt relieved that all was OK, and this was just the usual media hype. The beach and house were safe. That night, in the howling blackness, the real XXXL surge arrived in all its fury. Houses on the atoll got swept away, docks were ripped off their pilings, palm trees were uprooted, and entire *motu* were swept clean. Everyone in the Tuamotus worked through the night to save what they could.

The morning after dawned with *Fare* Fuller still standing. More photos were emailed. The damage was shocking. I was relieved yet heartbroken at the same time. The water surged up to our lanai and barely kissed one corner. It flowed to the right of the house and to the left of the house. It raged through our carport and under our boat. Salt water raced under the new gate we had just completed in the front of the carport and continued on toward the next house just inland of us. Later, surveying the damage, Rich and Scarlett agreed: It was a miracle that *Fare* Fuller had been spared.

My once-pristine beach was littered again with chunks of coral. Thick debris of every kind was left behind as the water receded over the next few days. Before I had a chance to get depressed, I got an email from William. He offered to have his adopted son, Laurent, conduct a massive cleanup for us. Laurent spent three solid days trying to make sense of the chaos. He cleaned out the carport and raked a bit of the beach. William, who has watched me sift sand tirelessly for the past four years, knew I'd come in and complete the final detail work. All I asked of Laurent was to save my *poitos*, fishing buoys. I'd amassed a nice collection over the years and used them as yard decorations.

After the initial shock, I pulled myself together. I asked Scarlett and Rich, now back from vacation, to look for a new wheelbarrow for me. Since everyone was in the same boat, I figured wheelbarrows might be a hot commodity on Rangiroa. Miraculously, they found one. It was green and smaller than the average wheelbarrow; however, it was a wheelbarrow, and I needed it. They stored it under their house until we arrived. I named her Pickle. Scooter managed to find some heavy-duty sifting boxes online. They were small, but mighty. We ordered two. Next up: a new sifting screen to cover Pickle's deep bed. I bought heavy-duty stretcher bars at the Kona art supply store (to be assembled later) and a roll of new wire screen at Lowe's. Armed with a few new sets of flexible work gloves, I was ready to rebuild the beach. Thankfully, everything fit inside our suitcases. I made a mental note to be ready to work once again in the sand.

We were pleasantly surprised when we first arrived. Yes, there was a lot of coral and debris; however, there were also abundant amounts of new, beautiful, sparkling sand. The sand had ridden in on the surge and miraculously managed to stay put. We were shocked to discover that we liked the new basic contour of the beach even better than before. By all means, there was work to do; howcvcr, our little area had the bones of a nice new beach in the making.

It took me one month to restore the beach. With Pickle by my side and new, improved sifting tools, it seemed to go faster than before. I used my previous "work experience" as my guide to efficiently create a beautiful beach. The *poitos* got repurposed and became ornaments in our *tou* tree. I must add that my rusty, old rake and blue ACE Hardware dustpan never let me down. Watching me work one day out on the beach, Teiva deemed me a "machine."

— *POSTSCRIPT* —

It takes approximately one week for the south swells to move from Tahiti to Hawaii. Everyone in Kona was poised and anxious, having seen footage from Tahiti's Code Red. When the swell arrived, I looked at Kaiwi Point and knew I'd better sit this one out. The waves in Kona were immense. There was a lot of carnage. One monster set even broke over the roof of a two-story waterfront condo.

A TRIP TO THE CITY

During our three-month rotation back in Kona, we make it a point to get all our medical and dental checkups. Any problems are addressed and, hopefully, resolved before we board our next flight to Tahiti. Teeth are cleaned and fillings are filled. Medications are reevaluated by primary care physicians and, if necessary, reordered with a three-month supply. Skin checks at the dermatologist are a regular must. Any suspicious spots are treated and need to be healed up before departure.

We carefully inventory our medical and first-aid kits before leaving Rangiroa. Both are extensive. Our Kona doctors know our story and have supported us by issuing prescriptions for just about any scenario that might arise while we're on the atoll. We amass and pack wound care items such as bandages, self-adhesive bandage wrap, sterile gauze pads, Steri-Strips, and prescription antibiotic cream in our suitcases.

Medical care on the atoll is very basic. There is a clinic

with a regular rotation of French doctors. There is also one private doctor. There is a dentist, and we've both found out that he's pretty good. The pharmacy is excellent. The pharmacist speaks English and takes her time when helping us. Many drugs here do not require a doctor's prescription. Serious medical problems or accidents require a trip to Papeʻete. If it's a medical emergency, Air Archipels, a subsidiary of Air Tahiti, flies in to pick up a patient for a "life flight" back to Tahiti. If we hear a plane fly over at night, we say, "Uh oh… wonder who got hurt?"

Bottom line: We do not want any medical issues while on Rangiroa. So far, it's gone well. We've been able to resolve anything that has arisen with local resources and our own supplies and medications.

During one trip, feeling confident that we had covered all of our medical and dental bases, we were at the gate in Kona, ready to begin our zigzag trek south. For no particular reason, I looked down at my arm. I saw something that made me seize up with worry. A very small spot had been frozen during my dermatology appointment one month prior. The spot was healing up nicely and normally. When I looked that morning, I saw a small bump in the middle of the light pink scar tissue. Uh oh, I thought, I know what that is. It was only the size of the head of a pin, but I was worried anyway.

Sure enough, that tiny bump grew during the first month we were on the atoll. I constantly stared at it and willed it to disappear. It was still very small, but I knew from experience that it needed to be removed. There were two choices: either pack it all in and return to Kona, or go to Papeéte and take a chance on an unknown dermatologist to treat it. I decided to get myself to Papeéte and get the spot taken care of.

I booked my flights, scheduled the doctor's appointment, and made hotel reservations. I had hoped to fly over in the morning, get to the appointment, and jump on an afternoon flight back to Rangiroa. Well, this is Tahiti, and things just don't work like that. There was a two-week school holiday, and students, families, and teachers were all on the move. There were very few flights to begin with, and all of them were booked solid. There was no other choice: I had to spend three days in a place I disliked immensely, Papeéte.

Before I left, Scarlett translated some information I wanted to tell the doctor in case she did not speak English. I contacted an acquaintance in Papeéte who was ready to assist me if I needed her. I packed a small carry-on bag and boarded the flight, choking back tears as I climbed up the stairs to the plane. I did not want to leave our beautiful, peaceful paradise. Scooter stayed behind to hold down the fort and to keep an eye on our boat, which was tied to two coconut trees in the *hoa*.

On the flight over, I made a new friend, Coco, Meho's cousin. She lives in the serene village of Tiputa, just across the pass. We were seatmates, and we spent the entire flight getting to know each other, speaking only Tahitian. She was on her way to see her doctor and *advocat* (attorney). She had been hit by a drunk driver while playing a game of *boules* on a street in Puna'auia (a district of Pape'ete) ten years ago. She has suffered since then from chronic knee pain. She then told me that her husband had been killed in the same accident. Now I was crying again, not for myself, but for her.

My hotel was nice enough. My Pape'ete friend suggested it because it is centrally located and close to the doctor's office. I felt safe and was comfortable in my room. After getting settled, I decided to take a walk. I wanted to scout out the doctor's office, maybe get a small bite to eat, find a book I wanted at a nearby bookstore, and possibly look at Polynesian apparel.

Out on the street, I did not feel safe. I quickly got lost and gave up on doing anything that was not totally necessary. The city is excessively noisy and extremely filthy. Sidewalks (if you call a thin strip of uneven asphalt a sidewalk) were crowded with wandering homeless people and their dogs. Thousands of cars were either gridlocked at street corners or racing at breakneck speed to the next gridlocked intersection. Walking beside so many maniacal cars was dangerous. Did I mention there are no street signs anywhere? Finding anything halfway healthy to eat was impossible. I'm no prude and have done my fair share of third-world traveling, but Pape'ete really made my skin crawl. Maybe my reaction was extreme due to the idyllic cocoon I'm used to on a remote coral atoll. In my mind, I'd gone from heaven to hell all in one day.

Except for my doctor's appointment, a facial appointment, a trip to the corner pharmacy, and a surprise stop at Moana's office, I basically hung out in my hotel room for the remainder of my stay. Being sedentary and cooped up inside is so far removed from my basic makeup. I like to move, do stuff, go places, meet people, have fun, and experience new things. When I can't do any of those things, I just shut down. On top of that, I got some bug, something like a mild flu, which had me shivering with fever.

The doctor was competent and did an excellent job for me. She spoke no English, so that cheat sheet Scarlett made for me was a lifesaver. As always, we made communication work with a mixture of hand gestures, voice intonations, and my fractured French. After I paid at her front desk, I was surprised to have the nurse hand me a small, sealed cup. Inside was my excised spot floating happily in a sterile solution. I was told (in French) that it was my responsibility to get that skin sample to the main medical lab. When I explained that I didn't know where I was going and that there were no street signs in their city, they simply shrugged their shoulders the way French people do and proceeded to print up a little generic Google map for me to follow. I already knew I was not going to blindly try to find my way on the streets of Pape'ete to an unknown destination several kilometers away with a sloshing cup in my hand.

Thankfully, my kind friend offered to help me out the next morning. She'd pick me up at my hotel, drive me to the main lab, and then continue and get me to the airport for my flight to Rangiroa.

I was packed up, checked out, and ready to go the next morning. She picked me up, and we were off to the main lab. My friend, a lifelong resident of Pape'ete, got lost and had to circle several blocks going up and down numerous one-way streets until we finally made it to the lab. She helped me get my sloshing sample handed in. I found out that all samples from Tahiti get shipped to France, where they can be analyzed. I've never been to France, but I can now say that a very small piece of me has.

I could not wait to fly out of Pape'ete and back to Scooter and our shared Shangri-La, our slice of paradise, a place of tranquil beauty. I had the last seat on the last flight of the day. Rangiroa was only a few hours away. I knew I would make it in one piece; however, there was one more little treat in store for me: our flight was delayed by two hours. Ah, Tahiti, what more can I say?

Once again, I made a new friend. As I sat at the gate in a hot, sticky seat, sipping a complimentary Sprite, I started a conversation in Tahitian with the small, white-haired Chinese man seated next to me. He was sweating and sipping, too. He was someone I'd never met, but someone I had wanted to meet. Bruno is the retired air traffic controller for Rangiroa. When he explained where he lived, I lit up like a Christmas tree. He lives just down the road from us. His house is my favorite house in all of Rangiroa. I pass it every day and have always wondered who lived there. I have admired it for years. It is two stories, dark brown, with very stylish architecture. It holds a bit of mystery because it's hidden partially by feathery *'aito* trees. His house is situated on the *hoa* where we moor our boat. It's an ideal location because he can see both the lagoon and the ocean from his second-floor lanai. Recently, I noticed a new addition to Bruno's *fare*: a tree house. It matches the main house with the dark brown paint and unique style. Chatting with Bruno made the delay bearable.

I practically ran off that plane after it came to a stop and the doors opened. Scooter was waiting for me, and, I admit, I cried again. This time my tears were tears of joy and relief. We jumped on the Vespa and zipped home, my little carry-on bag stashed on the running board between his feet. Sitting on our lanai a few minutes later, we were sipping rum drinks and watching the sun set over the lagoon. It took about three days for me to decompress and get my groove back. All that I know for sure is that I hope to never have to do that again.

— *POSTSCRIPT* —

My arm has healed beautifully. I had to keep it dry for about ten days. Staying dry is a huge challenge for me. I could swim, but that arm had to stay afloat on a life preserver.

I never got the results from the lab in France.

PATENT PENDING

There are only a few things I miss while living on a coral atoll in the South Pacific. This list is short as most everything I love about life is right here. I don't miss these things every day, just sometimes. I'm learning that life has trade-offs. I can certainly live with that.

First and foremost, I miss having easy access to talk with friends and family. I now know how to use Skype and Messenger, so that issue is slowly resolving. While I can make outgoing calls to people, calling me is difficult because we must have our *vini* box (Wi-Fi) on to receive calls. The *vini* box works very well; however, we pay by the gigabyte, and it is expensive. We turn the box on only when we need to access the Internet. Communicating takes a bit of coordination on both ends, but it is doable these days. Staying in touch with home means a lot to me, especially in a place where we are, and always will be, foreigners.

I miss good avocados. We can get avocados; unfortunately,

they are not nearly as flavorful as the avocados off the trees gracing our Kona yard. Fresh fruit and vegetables arrive from the Marquesas on the *Aranui*. The ship calls every ten days. Buying freshies off a cargo ship is harrowing, to say the least. Hard-muscled workers off-load produce and pile it all on a flat barge. They transport the highly sought–after cargo across the lagoon and then tie up at one of the docks to sell directly to throngs of waiting Rangiroans. Which dock? Nobody ever knows. We simply watch through our binoculars to see where the barge is headed. Then we know. We hope to get there before everyone else. Have your Tahitian French francs ready and be prepared to do battle with a tight knot of people all clambering to get the attention of the hawkers standing knee-deep in produce on the barge. Lately, we have skipped that drama and gone to Kamalita's fruit stand set up on the roadside in Avatoru Village. Kamalita has a standing order from the *Aranui*. Her order of fruits and vegetables is delivered directly to her on boat day. She sets everything up under her shady thatch and is open for business all day. It's a bit pricier, but way easier than doing battle dockside. If any avocados have been shipped, and if you are lucky enough to get one, be prepared for a watery, tasteless, and disappointing batch of guacamole.

I miss my dishwasher. I have lived most of my adult life without a dishwasher. When we designed and built our home, I said no to a dishwasher as we finalized the kitchen layout. About ten years later, on a surf trip to Australia, we experienced dishwashing drawers in the house we rented. For some reason, after that, I could not live without those dishwashing drawers. I redesigned our kitchen, bought and installed the drawers, and bam, I was in dishwashing heaven. I've learned how to do dishes Paumotu style with just cold water in the tap, a hot water kettle in the ready position, and a little container in the sink with a soapy sponge. Everyone I know here uses this method, with slight variations from household to household. I've gotten used to this system. It's efficient and uses water sparingly. The dishes are clean, but not that clean, especially if there is any grease involved. Even though this method works well enough, about two months into our stay, I seem to start longing for those sparkling dishwashing drawers and the immaculate dishes they produce.

But one of the key items that I miss dearly is my clothes dryer. Don't get me wrong, I love the freshly dried clothes from the line that we have in Rangiroa. It's energy-efficient and just a nice, natural way to do things. That is, if everything goes as planned. Grab a cool drink to sip, and I'll tell you all a story about doing laundry on a coral atoll.

As mentioned earlier, we are Mr. and Mrs. MacGyver. We must be. As problems arise, we need to figure out how to solve them using very limited resources, two feeble brains, and a trial-and-error approach. The problem: drying laundry. This is an age-old, worldwide chore. Nothing new. People wear clothes, wash clothes, dry clothes, and wear them again.

I've never given this notion much thought until we began to live on an atoll. In Kona, I'd toss a load in the washer, go work out, come home, toss the soggy clothes into the dryer, go surf, and come home once again, greeted by a batch of soft, fluffy, DRY clothes. It's just so easy. Life goes on, and laundry gets done without skipping a beat of a normal day. Doing laundry on a coral atoll very often can be an all-day extravaganza. There may be some stress, possibly a lot of high-speed sprinting, and the need to become a part-time meteorologist.

When we first moved in, we immediately strung up a new clothesline. The line left by the previous tenants was a combination of rusted wire, dilapidated cordage, and moldy twine. It sure felt good to pull that mess down and dump it in the trash can. The new clothesline stretched the entire length of our covered carport, with an upper and lower line. We also stretched a third line about one foot to the inside. Scooter is good with ropes and knots. He created a very functional clothesline that is also a work of art.

Our washer is new. It produces nice, clean clothes. We're fortunate to have this washer, and we treat it with kid gloves. When the wash cycle is done, I shuttle the wet clothes out to the carport and plop them on the picnic table. I then proceed to hang them up the way everyone else does, with clothespins.

The drying process works very well if I get it on the line by six thirty in the morning and if the weather is dry with a nice breeze blowing. No problem. On a day like that, clothes are dry by noon or before. Case closed. If it's a nice warm day, and no wind is blowing, the drying time is longer. If it's a cloudy day with wind, there could be issues. If it's a cloudy day with no wind, we've got a problem. If it's a rainy day, wind or no wind, forget doing laundry. Even if it's the perfect day to do laundry and the clothes are dry as a bone by noon, a fast-moving black cloud could magically appear, and the rain and wind could blow moisture on the previously perfectly baked batch of clothes. And back to the starting blocks we go.

After about three years here, we rigged up the Turbo Dryer. I can't believe it took us so long to figure this out. The Turbo Dryer consists of two lines of cord tied between the kitchen window and a tree. This clothesline is in direct sunlight. Things dry almost instantly if there are no clouds anywhere to be seen. If a black, moist rain cloud surprises us blowing in from the east, it's time to sprint, grab everything like a whirling dervish, and get it under the roof of the carport without dropping it all in the sand. The other concern with our Turbo Dryer is, I believe, that atoll rats can use the line as a direct freeway into our kitchen. Scooter disagrees. Teiva and Meho have seen the acrobatic feats of these rats and tend to agree with me.

Now, onward to tell you about my ingenious invention: 3D clothes drying. I'm so proud of myself for figuring this out. I'm positive that I could get a patent, sell millions, and become a bona fide billionaire. One day, about three weeks ago, I was staring at my running gear on the line, willing it to dry. It'd been a rough laundry day, which, during the wet season from November to March, was becoming more frequent. About 95 percent of our atoll clothes are made of lightweight, quick-dry material. Two items I use every day, unfortunately, are not: my running shorts and jog bra. Since I go for a daily early morning run, the shorts and bra need to be dry each afternoon. I have backup running gear; however, it's a point of honor for me to get my favorite outfit dry and ready for the next day's workout. As I stared at the limp, damp shorts and bra at about three in the afternoon, I asked myself, "How can I make this stuff dry faster?" I started fiddling with the clothespins, trying to separate the cloth a bit so that air would flow in and around the shorts and bra, and, voilà, I figured out a method of using the clothespins to spread the shorts and bra wide so that any puff of wind would do the job a lot faster than if they were simply hanging. I had "invented" 3D clothes drying. It has worked every day since, even if it's a damp day. It worked so well that we tried the method out on another problem item: bed sheets. To spread out the flat and fitted sheets 3D style, we used a broom and mop handle to separate the cloth for better airflow and drying capabilities. The mop handle was easily held in place with tension from the weight of the large amount of cloth.

I wondered if other people do 3D drying. I'm sure

they must. I've just never heard of it. I showed Scarlett the method recently when she was here for an afternoon game of Yahtzee. Scarlett has lived in Rangiroa for more than thirty years. She has hung laundry the entire time, and had an abundance of washing to do when she owned a small hotel out on a distant *motu*. She was intrigued as I demonstrated the simple steps. I first stretch the garment as far as it can go, using a wooden clothespin at both ends to hold it firmly in place. Next, I prop the clothespin up (using the tension created by stretching) to hold the front side of the garment out and as far away as possible from the back side of the garment. When propped up on the line, it looks as if there's an invisible person inside the 3D-hung item. Anyway, my idea works, and it has revolutionized my clothes-drying efforts.

As I type, there is a huge storm raging outside. Thunder, lightning, and buckets of rain are holding us hostage inside the house. As usual, I had my laundry hung, 3D style, before six thirty in the morning. The day had looked promising and had all the makings for an easy-drying day. I just looked out the window. Everything on the line is soaked, lying on the ground, or twisted up in a soggy knot on the clothesline. So much for my theories on clothes drying.

— POSTSCRIPT —

Please note: only the strength and stability of good, old-fashioned wooden clothespins work for 3D drying.

You may wonder why I opted for no dishwasher when we built our home in Kona. I'm convinced that I had a bit of post-traumatic stress disorder after growing up in a house where the dishwasher had frequent fits. The family would be quietly settled in after dinner, when, boom, the dishwasher running the dinner dishes would go kablooey. Dad would jump up from his reading chair, fling off his glasses, curse up a blue streak, grab a flashlight and some wrenches, and storm outside to clean out the pipes to get the dishwasher running once again.

OUR GHOST

When Laurent did the cleanup for us after the XXXL Storm of the Century, I asked him to set aside all our *poitos* (fishing buoys). They were precious to me given that I had collected so many over the years to use as yard art. At that time, I had been so busy rebuilding our beach that I had barely noticed that no buoys were anywhere to be seen. I figured either he had forgotten my request, or they had all ridden the surge back out into the lagoon, ending up as somebody else's yard art. After a month of beach work, William casually mentioned that all our *poitos* were tied up in his tree for safekeeping. He wondered if I still wanted them. I peeked around the *ni'au* (palm frond) fence, and, sure enough, there they were. And yes, I still wanted them.

Poitos are a big feature throughout all the Tuamotus. Pearl farmers use the colorful buoys to mark the location of their oyster cages. Those oysters grow dazzling black pearls. Pearl farming is both a big business and a way of life here.

There are hundreds and hundreds of oyster cages submerged in the Rangiroa lagoon. That means there are hundreds and hundreds of *poitos* floating in the lagoon directly above those cages. Thankfully, the pearl farming zone is restricted to one area, leaving the rest of this immense lagoon open, free of buoys, and natural for all to enjoy.

Poitos are also used for boat moorings. When used in that way, the buoy holds up a chain or rope that is attached to some sort of heavy weight deep below on the sandy bottom of the lagoon. Locals and visiting vessels depend on these moorings to keep their boats in one place.

Small foam *poitos* are also used as fenders. Tie one off to the side of your boat so that it cushions a bump to the boat jostling in the waves right next to you. People are considerate around here about putting fenders out to protect boats from causing any damage to another person's boat.

Commercial fishermen outside in the open ocean use *poitos* to hold up their nets and fishing lines. In the old days, these floats were made of blown glass. A glass blower would ride along with the fishermen on ocean-going vessels. As the fishermen drank their sake, the glass blower would use the empty bottles to create glass floats.

All of these buoys have a job. The swell action of the ocean sometimes rips a buoy free from its work site. Naturally, it floats on the surface of the water and eventually lands somewhere. People find the buoys wherever they land. I think of it a bit like an Easter egg hunt. It is exciting to find one—well, at least it is for me.

In Rangiroa, many people use these found "treasures" to decorate their houses and yards. Some people paint them to coordinate with the color of their house. Some people cut them in half and add macramé rope to create hanging planters. Some people hang them from the eaves of their houses. Some people use the *poitos* to perfectly cap their fences. Some *poitos* decorate mailboxes, and some decorate storefronts.

Poitos come in many shapes, sizes, and colors. They remind me of a box full of Christmas ornaments. Most are about the size of a basketball, although some are a bit smaller, and some can be a little larger. Some have intricately tied rope around them, creating a net. That rope work is a dying art. If you find one of those, do not mess with the net. It is a keeper just as it is. *Poitos* are made of plastic. I had a tough time grasping this fact because they are very heavy and hard, and they feel like they are made of metal.

Now that you know a lot about *poitos,* I need to tell you about our ghost, or as the Tahitians say, our *tupapa'u*. So, warm up a hot cup of tea or a steaming mug of coffee to slowly sip while I share the following story. Scooter preferred a cold beer or shot of whiskey after listening to me read and reread this chapter aloud to him while we were cooped up inside at our kitchen table as a storm raged outside.

One lazy atoll day, Scooter and I untied the *poitos* from William's tree and transferred them to our beach. There were fourteen in all. I laid them out in the sand to admire them and then used their wide variety of characteristics to sort them out under our *tou* tree. I was getting ready to hang them up and wanted a visual of what we had to work with. I excitedly told Scooter, "It's going to be just like putting ornaments on a Christmas tree!" He remained skeptical and just shook his head as I was getting increasingly excited about this project.

We moved our wobbly, termite-infested picnic table out to the beach. The table has become our "Paumotu ladder" since the one Moana has is a French version that we cannot figure out. We worked together as a team: me, The Director of Ornament Hanging, and Scooter, The Rope and Knot Guy. I called upon my Christmas tree decorating lessons my dad had taught me way back when. I can still hear him instruct me year after year to "vary the heights of the ornaments and vary the color and shape of them, too." So, that's just what I did. Thankfully, Scooter is a wizard with ropes and knots. He devised a method using a fishing weight along with our "Paumotu tree trimmer" to loop the rope over some of the higher branches. I'd stand back and analyze the perfect height for each *poito*. He would adjust the rope higher or lower, then tie it off with skill. Hanging those fourteen *poitos* was fast and easy. Before we knew it, that picnic table was back in the carport, and we had our very own *tumu poito 'ori'ori*, dancing buoy tree.

A few days later, I found another *poito*. Then Scarlett and Rich delivered a few more. After that, I found one more in the *hoa* on my early morning run. Soon we had twenty beautiful balls hanging from the branches. It really did look like a Tahitian Christmas tree. I was enraptured by the view and could not stop admiring the tree's colorful beauty.

One of the buoys that Scarlett brought over was round, black, and in perfect condition. It was the style of *poito* that has two "ears" (line loops) on top. She found that one in the *hoa* behind her house. It was wrapped up in a massive tangle of branches that flowed in after the XXXL Storm of the Century. At first, she didn't think she could get it out. She changed her mind and tried again, this time finding success.

Scooter took one look at that big black ball with two ears and decided to draw a kitty cat face on it with white paint. Given that it wasn't my style at all, I didn't really like the idea. I love the *poitos* as they are—just natural. A kitty cat face would detract from the "overall flow of beauty," or some such nonsense I came up with as my case against that kitty face. Scooter prevailed. The next day, he got out the paint set and a small brush. He sat down at the picnic table, then took his time with his kitty creation. I must admit, he did an excellent job, and I liked the face, but I was still against the idea of a kitty face up in the tree. I guess you might say I had a bad attitude about that cat. After we hung that *poito* up, for some reason, that kitty cat face with the yellow eyes kept staring directly at me, or so it felt like. Just like Pinocchio, the wooden puppet, that *poito* had somehow found life, and I was the villain of the story by trying to prevent its birth. Nevertheless, the kitty cat became a part of the *tumu poito 'ori'ori.*

A few days later, it was Halloween. We woke up to a bright, sunny day. Unfortunately, by seven in the morning, the atoll bliss was interrupted by the faint smell of death. Sure enough, we found a dead cat in the side yard, under the *poito* tree. It was a beautiful cat, fluffy and healthy looking. We were sure the roaming dogs had gotten it. Scooter had to scoop it up and take it to the coconut forest for burial. It was unsettling. We love cats and, sadly, had lost our own cats, Pepper and Salty, to marauding Paumotu dogs about a year before.

That Halloween evening, something very strange happened. We were enjoying dinner together at the table in our kitchen. As always, the bifold doors to the beach were wide open. There was not a breath of wind. Everything was still as could be. I looked up as the sun was setting and noticed, out of the corner of my eye, the black kitty cat *poito* was swinging wildly in the tree. No other buoy was moving at all, not even a fraction of an inch. We both stared at the cat. As it swung back and forth, back and forth, those yellow eyes looked right into my blue eyes without wavering once. We got up from dinner and went out to look closer. We looked to see if a rat or a gecko was running around on that branch. We looked everywhere to see why that kitty cat was swinging and why it was the only *poito* on the move. We couldn't see any reason that would logically explain why that demon of a cat continued to swing on and on. Scooter took a video of the action, just to document it for anyone doubting our sanity. We watched and watched, shaking our heads in disbelief.

The swinging of just that one *poito* got wilder as each minute passed. After an hour of observation, we decided to call it a day. We closed the house down and turned off the lights. When I finally shut the door, I looked one last time. That black ball with the kitty cat's face was still swinging. A while later, after trying to fall asleep, I was still bewildered by that cat. I got up, grabbed my flashlight, and went outside into the dark night. I walked barefoot in the soft sand to the *tou* tree only to see that the kitty cat was finally still. Now no buoy moved a fraction of an inch. All was well once again at *Fare* Fuller on that Halloween night.

Tahitians believe in ghosts. Feeling and seeing spirits all around is common here. It is a big part of legend, lore, and life. Almost every house leaves a light on all night, just above the door. Even Teiva and Meho mounted the gaping jaws of a big shark just above their entry. When I asked him about it, he simply said one word, "*Tupapa'u*." I am not sure if I believe in ghosts or not. For now, the swinging cat with the yellow eyes is all that I can handle.

NEW NEIGHBORS

Here at Moana's Village, there's a very good vibe. There are four households on Moana and Tarona's land. Their parcel stretches from the road all the way to the lagoon. There's a long, winding sand driveway, a few patches of grass, and many coconut palms. Although the houses are close together, the placement of each structure gives us each a good measure of privacy. The thick vegetation and *ni'au* fences add even more privacy. Moana's Village is surrounded by open land on three sides, and the vast lagoon on the fourth.

Currently, our little bubble feels like a real community where people help and care about each other. Everyone here is considerate, friendly, and quick to pitch in with work. We gather for sunset cocktails and often share the bounty of fresh fruits and vegetables. It makes such a difference having a good energy environment. Last year, there was a family here that was inconsiderate. I'll take the high road and leave it at that. They only stayed one year. They moved on to a bigger house in the village of Avatoru.

Up by the road live François and Jeanne. She's the French teacher at the local *collège* (junior high school), and he is an "on-call" driver for a few of the small hotels. They are here on a four-year teaching contract. In France, François explained, he was "like an air traffic controller for the railway system." Jeanne is petite, blond, and very attractive. I find it amazing that she can maintain a well-put-together appearance in this extreme atoll environment. François is dark haired and handsome. He is constantly raking his beach, creating artful projects, and beautifying their yard and house. François and Jeanne are striving to learn English. We are attempting to improve our French. We had them over for sunset cocktails about a week ago. Scarlett and Rich were also here. Scarlett helped us when we got stuck in a conversation. It went well.

Recently, François came over to visit. He brought a gift for us: a cool sign he had designed and made. It's on a palm stalk and says, "KONA 2452 MI." There's an arrow, too, indicating the direction. Before he came over, he told us he checked Google to see how to say, "You are nice neighbors," so that he could relay his sentiments. We feel the same about François and Jeanne. Now, where can we hang that sign? It needs to be pointing to the northwest, to Kona, Hawaii.

The middle house has our new neighbors, a very nice young family. They are French but have been living in Santiago, Chile, for the past eight years. They are also here on a four-year teaching contract. Joa, the dad, is the PE teacher at the *collège*. He's a bundle of fun energy and thrives on extreme sports activities. He could be a model, and, of course, he is very fit. Charlie, a primary school teacher, is currently an at-home mom caring for their youngest child. Charlie could not be nicer. She is dark haired, has a huge smile, and radiates true and calm beauty. Their son, Noam, is five. He is sweet, soft spoken, and introspective. He's an observer. He takes his time to carefully look at things on the beach and in the lagoon. He's attending school here. I assume his grade is equivalent to our kindergarten level. Then there's Tara, their two-year-old daughter. Scooter used the word "enchanting" the other day to describe her. It's the only time I've ever heard him use that word. It's the perfect descriptor for this tiny, cosmic ball of sparkling energy.

Tara just turned two a few months ago. She fears nothing. We've seen her climb tall trees, try to "get air" on her little wooden push bike by zooming down a miniramp in their garage, concentrate on fishing with a long bamboo pole at the edge of the lagoon, climb up and down huge coral boulders, paddle a stand-up paddleboard on her own, and cling to her dad's back when he snorkels way, way out in the lagoon. It appears as if Tara feels everything with more emotion than normal human beings. When she cries, she cries with unbridled abandon. When she laughs, it's with all her being. When exploring, moving, or doing everything that a "normal (just) two-year-old" would never attempt, it is all out or not at all. One day, I went to talk with Charlie. Tara had on a tiny helmet and was pretending to "rock climb" up the front of the family washing machine. We love watching her, and are always amazed at what this three-foot, golden-haired, complete package of a human being does.

The middle house belonging to Joa and Charlie is a home where great love and happiness reside. Watching this family live life as it should be lived is an inspiration. They do not have a TV. While they do have a computer, it's reserved for kid use only on rainy days. Joa handcrafted an adventure playground for the kids out in the coconut forest. He cleared a long, meandering bike track through the dense foliage. He "paved" the course with small coral pieces. There is a START and FINISH line. He also hung up a set of Tarzan swings. Recently, I noticed that he'd stretched a tightrope between two sturdy palms. Instead of sitting in front of a mind-numbing blue screen, this family goes out and experiences all that this beautiful world has to offer. Hats off to them.

The next household is *Fare* Fuller. We have seniority at Moana's Village, having been here for four years. We are also the oldest residents (by far). We are unique in that we're only here part-time, speak very little French, and are not teachers at the *collège*. In a way, these factors separate us from everyone else. Sometimes we feel like outsiders. We have very happily gone overboard in being kind, generous, and helpful to our neighbors to compensate for being unable to communicate readily in French. Our home is a place of laughter, fun, and ongoing geriatric adventures.

Next door is William, the unofficial mayor of Moana's Village. He's in his midfifties. He has taught French history at the *collège* for many years. All through his life, he has *fa'a'amu-ed* (adopted) many young people. He explained that he was adopted as a young child, and he wants to do the same to help others. He is Tahitian and originally from the rural district of Taravao on the island of Tahiti. He readily helps me with my Tahitian, introduces us to local foods, and demonstrates how to create beautiful things out of leaves, palm fronds, and flowers. His yard and beach are adorned with handmade creations hanging from trees and artfully placed in the sand. He has many nice friends who join him at the picnic table under his thatched *fare pote'e*. Those friends have morphed into our friends as the years have gone by. William epitomizes the heart and soul of a Tahitian.

Fare Fuller and William's *fare pote'e* are situated on the beach. We each have a sandy yard and direct access to the lagoon. François and Jeanne and Joa and Charlie have both carved out their own beachfront areas just to the west. François has worked tirelessly to get their area all set up with chairs, loungers, and hammocks. He is currently working on a fence of sorts, using wild tree branches. Joa has been developing his family's area as well. He built a shady hut made of palm branches, sifted a big circle of sand for his kids to play in, created tables and chairs with scrap lumber, and cleared some coral in the lagoon to make a small swimming pool.

Scooter and I hope that nobody moves to upset the perfect

balance of personalities here in Moana's Village. We were relieved a few days ago when Joa spontaneously said, "This is the best area in all of Rangiroa." It really is the ideal spot. We were elated when William recently mentioned that after retirement he plans to stay in his *fare pote'e*. It's perfect for him. We were happily surprised when François and Jeanne told us that they were only in year two of a four-year contract. Previously, we thought it was a three-year obligation. Yay! As for the Fullers, our lease will be up in another year. We plan to stay on as long as we are physically able to meet the daily challenges of atoll living and as long as Tarona and Moana will have us.

THANKSGIVING ON AN ATOLL

I was a kindergarten teacher for years. Every November, I taught the little guys and girls all about Pilgrims, Native Americans, and the feast. We also studied food groups at that time. Every year, on the Wednesday before Thanksgiving, I organized a classroom feast. We laboriously made costumes. Each child could choose between a Pilgrim hat and collar, or an Indian headdress and vest. On that Wednesday, everyone arrived at school dressed up in anticipation of enjoying lunch together in our classroom. It really was fun. Every year, I dressed up as a Pilgrim. Not because I wanted to, but because I just happened to have a long black dress in my closet, a long white apron in a kitchen drawer, and a big poofy chef's hat out by our barbecue. I figured out that if I folded down and then flipped up the brim of the chef's hat, it, amazingly enough, looked just like those very ugly women's Pilgrim hats you see in all the artist's renditions.

One November, we had house guests from Tahiti staying at our place in Kona. I arrived home that Wednesday after the classroom minifeast. I was still in my Pilgrim getup. I parked my car at the top of our driveway and proceeded to walk casually down to the house, exhausted from a busy school day. My friends, who happened to be at the bottom of the drive, looked up to see a black and white vision of ugliness—me. They froze with horrified expressions on their faces. Carol, a wearer of bikinis, *pareus* (Tahitian sarong), and rubber slippers, was somehow transformed into something they did not understand: a Pilgrim in a floppy, oversized white hat. They knew absolutely nothing about Thanksgiving, Pilgrims, Native Americans, or the famous feast. I will never forget the look on their faces and how hard we all laughed. After recovering from all that laughter, I tried to give them a nutshell version of Thanksgiving, and in doing so, explain my odd appearance.

There are exactly two expat Americans here in Rangiroa. There's Scarlett, my best friend, and there's Waiapa. Scarlett, originally from Ohio, made it to the atoll via Kauai and Big Sur, California. Waiapa, with his Hawaiian blood, lived most of his early life in Northern California and made his way to Rangiroa via the world of Polynesian dancing and drumming. Scarlett and Waiapa are married to locals, have lived here for years, and are fully assimilated into atoll life. Then there are the Fullers, here for one half of each year. That makes just four people who have firsthand knowledge about Thanksgiving.

For everyone else in Rangiroa, that Thursday in late November is just another ordinary tropical day.

Last year we decided to have an impromptu feast with Scarlett and Rich on the appointed Thursday. We just happened to have two freeze-dried Mountain House backpackers' turkey dinners. The pouches consist of a "glop" made with small turkey bits, freeze-dried peas and carrots, a bit of fake gravy, and a little stuffing. Just add one cup of hot water, reseal the pouch, wait five minutes, and—presto—Thanksgiving dinner is complete. Rich made an instant potato concoction because real potatoes were nowhere to be found on the atoll at that time. We had a side of Stove Top stuffing, and I whipped up a creamed carrot/coconut milk dish to round things out. I set the picnic table with my best silverware, nice linen, and clean place mats. We lit candles to set the mood. Scarlett and I shared in the purchase of a nice bottle of French champagne. Scarlett and Rich arrived with the potatoes, the bottle of bubbly, and a large wooden box. Inside the box was a set of the most magnificent champagne flutes I'd ever seen. They were crystal, ornately carved, extremely delicate, and so incongruous with sand, coral, and palm trees. We ate our feast as if we were dining at the Four Seasons. Everyone else in Moana's Village just went on with an ordinary Thursday as we clinked those champagne flutes over and over, making toasts to this and that. The dessert was ice cream and chocolate chip cookies. All in all, the meal wasn't too bad. We had a fun time with good friends, and that's all that counts.

After dinner, as the conversation continued, Scarlett and I thought that next year we might try to cook a real turkey. It is possible to buy one here with some advance planning. Scooter and Rich just stared at the lagoon as Scarlett and I grew more excited and animated about the idea. Or maybe it was just me getting more excited about this idea. I'm not sure.

Over the coming year, I kept thinking about how to pull off a real Thanksgiving dinner on an atoll. Turkey could be ordered through Magasin Daniel. Scarlett has worked in their back office for years. She knows firsthand how to get things done around here. We would make sure to pack more Stove Top stuffing and a few cans of cranberry sauce in our suitcases. Potatoes can usually be found here. We would all be on the lookout for those well in advance. I could recreate the creamed carrot dish. Scarlett offered to make a pie, provided she could find some sort of premade baking crust imported from France.

As November arrived, we all talked about the upcoming feast. Each of us looked high and low in the stores for what we would be needing. We compared notes on who saw what at which store. The weekend before Thanksgiving, we had a small dinner party planned. As I was preparing for that, Scooter confessed that he had reservations about hosting two events in one week. He had a point. I'm not the best cook, and preparing food here is hard work, so we compromised: we'd have our dinner party and cancel Thanksgiving. I could live with that. The small dinner party morphed into a mock

Thanksgiving feast a week early with a modified menu. Instead of turkey, I made an all-American meatloaf. I also filled halves of colorful bell peppers with Stove Top stuffing. Scarlett brought deviled eggs, and Rich made a beautiful salad of grated green papaya. Nua, our other guest, made one of her famous tarts. Rich and Nua had never eaten meatloaf or stuffing before. Rich knew little about Thanksgiving; Nua knew nothing. So, once again, the story was relayed. That part was easy. Trying to explain stuffing was a bit more difficult.

— *POSTSCRIPT* —

I have made those stuffed bell peppers a few more times. Once, we took them to Toriki and Manon's house to share at the dinner table, and then I served them at a casual block party at our house for all the Moana's Village crew. Nobody knows anything about stuffing, but everyone likes it.

WHO NEEDS A MIRROR?

Have you ever wondered what the dress code is for life on a coral atoll? It might sound utterly inconsequential, but, like so many other aspects of atoll life, it has taken its sweet time for us to adjust to what is acceptable attire here.

There are some people on the atoll who dress nicely. They have regular jobs and dress accordingly. Other people work with copra or commercial fish. Others are dive instructors or pearl divers. In those cases, clothes simply do not matter. The wind, rain, and incessant saltwater ruin clothing quickly, so why bother? Tourists dress nicely in resort wear. They are very easy to spot. Their clothes are clean, crisp, and colorful.

I usually take a bit of pride in my appearance. I schedule regular facials, waxings, manicures, pedicures, and hair treatments. While I'm no clotheshorse, I do like to dress presentably when zipping about Kona to do shopping, run errands, or meet friends for a casual lunch. Kona is pretty laid-back. Almost every day I wear the same thing: workout clothes before breakfast, a bikini over a T-shirt and shorts to go for a midmorning surf, and a nicer pair of shorts and top to run errands after lunch. Each evening, I tie on a Tahitian *pareu* after my shower. At each stage of my Kona day, I look presentable enough.

In Rangiroa, I simply do not care how I look. Scooter is the same. There is absolutely no reason to even be halfway presentable. Most days I never leave our house anyway. Our place has everything I love: an idyllic home full of refreshing breezes opened wide to the lagoon, a beautiful beach, and a turquoise-blue swimming hole right out front. I suit up in the morning, and that garb lasts all day. "Suiting up" begins with selecting a bikini from my bikini box in the bedroom. Not to be too personal, however, I will reveal at this point that the bikini acts as my underwear for the day. I can work, swim, and go fishing without missing a beat.

Bikini secured, next stop: the big woven basket in our carport. In that basket are all of our DCC (Designated Crappy Clothes). First, I pick out a pair of "shorts." Shorts are usually a pair of Scooter's cast-off PSD brand boxer briefs. To me, the PSDs just look like fun, colorful shorts. He has an enormous collection of them. He insists that it's huge only because he has a wife who regularly steals them. To be fair, I also have a few pairs of surf trunks in the big basket. I bought them at the Kona Target in the little boy's department. They fit, are durable, and dry quickly—all requirements of Rangiroa attire. Next, I pick out an old Columbia T-shirt, another Scooter cast-off. As he ruins those pricey Columbia tees while working with grease, paint, and lubricants, I rejoice because then they will go into the big DCC basket and become fair game for me. Thankfully, the Columbia shirt hangs down low on me and covers up that pouch on his "donated" underwear. Next up, my ugly Gilligan hat. It's a bucket hat just like Gilligan's. On him, it looked cute. On me, the hat is very unflattering. I've cut off the top of the hat so that my big bun of blond hair can stick out of the top. The big bun is held in place with a cheap wooden chopstick that Scooter sharpened with his pocket knife. It never fails to hold my hair in place as I toil away raking sand, trimming trees, moving coconuts, or taking off for some lagoon fishing in the boat. Before I begin the day's projects, I slather on a thick layer of zinc-based sunscreen. I call myself a *tupapa'u*, a ghost, because my skin is totally white from that zinc. The last addition to my outfit is the most important one of all: my white Crocs. These are four-wheel-drive footwear for atoll living and essential gear when the ground consists of coral and sand.

Most days I work happily away in our yard in this minimal but functional attire. Sometimes I need to ride my bike to the bank, *magasin*, or hardware store. When I do go out, I confess that I do not change into anything decent. I wipe off some of the zinc to a presentable level, replace the bucket hat with my orange, faded visor, and then I ride out on my bike just as I am. People here do not blink an eye. Nobody cares. Nobody notices. It's kind of cool to have no pressure to look a certain way.

You may remember that our bathroom appears to have been designed and built by giants. The mirror is high up on the wall. If you are 6'2", it's perfect. Scooter is 5'5", and I'm 5'1". When we moved in, we simply could not see ourselves unless we jumped up and down or stood on a stool. One of the first things we hauled down from Kona was a small, unbreakable mirror to prop up under the giant's mirror behind the sink. It's been propped up right there ever since. It's not a real mirror, so the reflection is a bit distorted, like the ones you'd see in a carnival sideshow. If I turn sideways, my stomach appears to poof out. Is that real or a consequence of too many baguettes?

The bottom line: I do not look in the mirror very often and have concluded that I do not even need a mirror. My daily raggedy outfit, the ghost-white face, and the clown hat are things I really don't care to see reflected back at me.

UNAUTHORIZED BIOGRAPHY

You already know my story of falling in love with Tahiti as a small child. I'm grateful every day that my parents introduced me to this beautiful world. I picked up the baton of their obsession and carried on with my own South Pacific adventures after they hung it up. None of my siblings got the Tahiti Disease. Just me. Much later I infected Scooter. Getting infected with something so beautiful and exotic is a wonderful thing. He has never complained about having the Tahiti Disease; in fact, his reaction has been quite the opposite.

Just who is this guy who has so seamlessly integrated himself into Tahitian life? Who is the man who puts up with all my antics, harebrained schemes, and (sometimes) out-of-bounds activities? I think of us as the real-life Lucy and Desi. I dream up stuff, and he puts up with all of it (most of the time) with a shake of his head. I'm not sure how he does it, but I'm sure glad we're sharing this adventure on a speck of sand in the middle of the South Pacific. Here's his Unauthorized Biography.

Scooter was born in Santa Maria, on the Central Coast of California. His family moved to Carson City, Nevada, when he was twelve years old. He spent his childhood exploring abandoned mining towns out in the vast sea of tumbleweeds. He and his dad wandered down winding dirt roads, scouring the desert for treasures in an old beat-up Jeep. When he reached his teens, he and his older brother both got into cars. Each brother would buy, sell, trade, and fix up classic cars and motorcycles. At one time, the two brothers had twelve cars in their collection. Each car was always on its way in or on its way out, an endless shuffle of steel, glass, and rubber.

With Lake Tahoe close by, Scooter became a water-skier in the summer and a snow-skier in the winter. He caught his first fish with a little kid's plastic rod and reel. It was a small bluegill. From that point on, he was hooked. He spent hours trout fishing in the lakes and streams around Tahoe for the remainder of his youth.

After four years in the US Navy, Scooter returned to Carson City and settled down as a family man. He and his wife had two small children. He became a fireman for the Carson City Fire Department.

After a divorce, he left Carson City behind and moved to Kona. It was the mid-1970s, and Kona was wide open. It had only one stoplight at that time. In Kona, he was able to reignite his passion for fishing. Crusty old boat captains took him under their wings to teach him the ropes of big-game fishing. He took any and all fishing-related jobs offered just to get the experience under his belt. Within one year, he became a charter captain in his own right. He had to climb the ladder like all the other captains. He started with small boats and worked his way up to the fancy, all-the-bells-and-whistle boats.

The next forty years found him at his "office," the helm of various charter boats in the fleet. He played host to a revolving door of anglers who were hoping to catch a marlin in Kona's renowned fishing grounds. He had a faithful following of clientele who returned year after year to try their luck. He worked very long hours out at sea almost every day. I'm not sure how he did it, but he also led the busy life of a single dad every summer when his two children came to stay with him.

The guys in Honokohau Harbor were a tight bunch of renegades, all choosing the path of life on the ocean. When he arrived, there were already two captains named Scott, so his handle became "Scooter" because he rode a Harley.

Scooter is an excellent conversationalist. That was the first thing I noticed about him when we met. He finely honed this skill as he entertained different clients every day aboard his charter boat. He knows how to tell a good story, and he's also a great listener. He's quick to laugh and find humor in just about any scenario. He's an easy-going guy, most of the time. He's very forgiving. If someone or something crosses him, he does get angry, but he gets over it quickly. He's also very humble and tends to be soft-spoken. When I told him about this chapter, he protested and said, "Oh no, it will be an *unauthorized* biography!"

Scooter's a guy's guy. He knows how to turn a wrench, fix things, has a lot of tools, and knows just about everything mechanical. He's the guy other guys call when they need help. As soon as anyone needs him, he's off, his truck bed loaded up with the appropriate tools the job might require. On the flip side, he rarely asks anyone for help. He usually just figures things out on his own in true MacGyver style.

He's artistic in that he's got a good eye for lines in the design of cars, boats, motorcycles, and all related equipment. Most of the time, he's got a great personal style. His day-to-day presentation in Rangiroa is like mine: pretty crusty. In Kona, he looks sharp every time he leaves the house.

He's a news junkie, reading online feeds for local, state, national, and international stories. He knows about everything going on everywhere. He relays his knowledge, and I take some of it in since I really don't care much for the news anymore. The cool part about us is that we are so different, yet we complement each other in so many ways. We make the best team for just about everything, especially navigating atoll life.

When we first met, naturally, I filled him in on all my solo Tahitian adventures. He had never been to Tahiti but had always wanted to go. He had several fishing buddies who had migrated to the South Pacific and had already relayed some tantalizing tidbits to him.

One summer, we were at the after-party for the Big Island Marlin Tournament. He caught the biggest fish in that competition on day one of the three-day event. That fish was enough to hold on to the lead until the end of day three. He and his team won first prize. First prize consisted of some good old-fashioned cash. With our usually empty pockets filled with bills, we immediately used that money to place a bid on a silent auction item: a three-day fishing charter in Raiatea aboard a 32-foot Blackfin, the *Tevaite*. We were the winning bid, so we came home that night with empty pockets and a certificate for some fun fishing in Tahiti.

The following December we went on our first trip to Tahiti as a couple. That trip was an all-time favorite! We met Ari and Hina, our hosts, and fished aboard their boat between Raiatea, Taha'a, and then all the way to Bora Bora. As a first-time Tahitian experience for Scooter, it simply could not have been any better. This was the moment that he got infected with the Tahiti Disease. Ever since then, we have explored the many corners of French Polynesia side by side before finally settling in Rangiroa.

Since I rarely care to leave our shack in the sand, Scooter is our goodwill ambassador out in the Rangiroa community. At first, I was the one who knew everybody and met people by the dozens, mostly because I used my basic Tahitian when we were out and about. As time has passed, he's been the one meeting all sorts of new people. Everybody is getting to know him. His genuine aloha spirit takes him a long way with the people here.

He's becoming well-known among the local fishermen and boat captains. Because he's a lifelong fisherman from Kona, the guys have really taken him in. He's one of them. He can speak some French and even more Tahitian, so the guys meet him halfway with whatever English they might know, but it really doesn't matter because they speak the universal language of fishing. He's been *e tua* (outside the lagoon in the open ocean) fishing for mahi-mahi with the *patia* (spear) with several local fishermen. This is a trial by fire, of sorts. Anybody who can deckhand on a *poti marara* (open-air Tahitian-style fishing boat) while basically riding rodeo on the rough water and spear a moving mahi has the Rangiroa Seal of Approval.

I simply cannot imagine my life here without my compadre. We are in total agreement: we do not want this amazing adventure to end anytime soon.

— *POSTSCRIPT* —

Scooter is known here in Rangiroa simply as Scott, his given name. For some reason, people do not like to use his nickname, Scooter. We're not sure why. Some people call him "Scotch." We're not sure why that is either.

Hina and Ari, from our Tevaite *days, remain some of our closest friends to this day. They have helped us in countless ways over the years. I am so glad we bid on that fishing trip at the silent auction all those years ago. They have proven to be the gold standard in the friendship department!*

A NEW DRIVEWAY

A while back Scooter asked me if I would use some coral rubble to build up a little berm where the concrete pad of our carport meets the sandy driveway. We were just about to pull *Vahine Iti* out of the water. Our regular three months on "Tahitian time" was coming to an end, and the boat needed to be cleaned, serviced, and put away. In our absence, she's covered up and secured in our carport. She fits perfectly.

Getting her backed into the carport is a challenge. The driveway into Moana's Village goes straight, then takes a hard left, then a sharp right to our carport. At first, Teiva tried to back her all the way to the concrete of the carport. That was met by a lot of tire grinding, missed attempts, and wildly differing ideas on how to get her in. As time passed, we got smarter. Now he backs her in straight from the road and parks her in front of William's house. We unhitch her at that point. From there, it's all hands on deck as we push and pull her to take those two turns. At the very end, we always have trouble getting up enough steam to push her over the little edge of the concrete and up into the carport. Back and forth, back and forth we'd push, rocking her to pick up momentum to be able to jump the curb. Finally, with all of us grunting, we'd get her over that one-inch bump and safely into the carport.

When Scooter asked me if I'd use some of the sifted-out coral rubble to create a berm at the edge of the carport, I was elated. I had been wanting to do something constructive with the small pieces of sifted-out coral, make something useful with them. I wasn't sure if the new coral berm would help or hinder the boat's access. Nevertheless, I got to work sifting, sorting, and transporting coral chunks to the front of the carport, one bucket at a time. I poured out small piles and spread the coral chunks out using my hands. Slowly, I worked my way across the entire width of the carport. When done, there was a nice ramp of sorts. It was only about two to three inches wide, but it looked hopeful.

Standing back, analyzing the little berm, I instantly fell in love with the new look. Previously, our driveway had been riddled with holes that turned into mud puddles after the rain. In addition, there were several large, half-buried boulders of coral that had me constantly stubbing my toe. This new look, reminiscent of mid-century modern xeriscapes, was clean and very inviting. It was at this point that I grabbed the rake and drew a line about five feet out in the dusty drive. That line was my goal for our new driveway.

Here I go again, I thought. I sure hoped it was not another

hornet's nest of ongoing hot, hard heavy work like the beach sand project. Just as I drew that line on the ground, beautiful, happy Charlie emerged from her house. She looked at the line and then at me standing there with my ragtag tools, planning my projected work. With gestures and my broken French, I tried to explain what I was doing. She just smiled and said, "*Bonne chance,*" which I knew meant "good luck" in French, and continued on, walking peacefully to the beach to take a swim.

Within a few days, the new driveway was complete. It certainly looked better. It was more welcoming and had much cleaner lines. Would the coral berm work, though? I wondered. On the appointed day, Teiva, Meho, and Scooter arrived with *Vahine Iti* on her trailer. As usual, we unhitched her, surrounded her with all of our helping hands, and started to push, pull, and grunt under the strain. Sure enough, the little berm leading up to the carport cement pad worked. Up and over she went as smooth as butter. Mission accomplished.

MARINE DEBRIS ARTIST

Before finally settling in our shack in the sand, we stayed at many different places in Rangiroa. One of our favorite spots was out on Tepu's *motu*. Her small island is located about thirty minutes to the east by boat. It is the quintessential picture-postcard setting one imagines when conjuring up a mental image of a South Pacific isle. We loved it out there in the sector. We rented her comfortable two-bedroom house, complete with a detached Tahitian kitchen. It was situated on the sand by the turquoise lagoon, but we could also look out to see the waves breaking on the outer reef. We would stay for no less than one month at a time and hunker down to live local style.

The term "sector" refers to all the *motu* not within the six-mile stretch between Avatoru and Tiputa Villages. The term is a reference to when copra was a major business in the Tuamotus. It is beautiful out in the sector; however, it takes Paumotu know-how to make *motu* living viable. Most houses in the sector are very basic. Some families use their sector house on weekends or holidays and for large family gatherings. Other people live full-time out in the tropical wilds. They can earn a meager living by working copra, stringing shell leis, or tending fish traps. A few very hearty souls have started vegetable gardening on their *motu*. How anything grows in sand and coral is something I have yet to comprehend. Some industrious people have started to rent out their *motu* to people like us who like a taste of something untamed. There are a handful of *motu* that have luxurious homes—something right out of a high-end travel brochure. Do not be fooled. Even the sumptuous homes on their very own *motu* requires a lot of work. I am over the phase when I would say to myself, "If I were really rich, I'd own my own *motu*." I know too much now about what that life entails.

As you can imagine, there is not much to do on a *motu*, unless you know how to make your own fun, dream up activities, and aren't afraid to try new things. It also helps to pack a few items that can be used to fill the long, dreamy days and moonlit nights. When packing my bag for Tepu's place, I would toss in a few small bottles of superglue, a few more bottles of white Elmer's glue, a small set of paints, and a wide variety of other craft items. The blistering days would find us in the cool shade of our open-air Tahitian kitchen. After exploring, swimming, and boating to the village for supplies, there was always time to create under the thatch.

From Tepu's bungalow on the languid lagoon, it was a short distance out to the pounding ocean reef. Scooter and I would walk out on the reef to explore and see nature at its finest. We would pick *ma'oa* (a gastropod) out of the swirling water to sauté in butter and garlic, look for *poitos,* and feel absolutely free and as far from civilization as possible. It is magnificent out there: birds screeching, waves crashing, every configuration of sand, sea, and sky, and not a soul for miles and miles. Walking along, enjoying nature takes on a mesmerizing feel—that is, until you happen upon the pieces of plastic marine debris that have washed in with the high tide.

All over the world, plastic refuse has become the bane of modern civilization. It is no different in Rangiroa. Plastic, whether carelessly discarded or accidentally dropped, often ends up in the ocean, and then it eventually comes to rest upon the shore. Not only is it unsightly, but it has also unfortunately become a part of the food chain as fish ingest the microplastic bits, thinking that they're food. Plastic marine debris is such a huge problem, one that depresses me if I think about it too much. I feel so small in the ongoing battle against plastic.

Walking along in nature at Tepu's, I could not help but pick up the glaring bits of plastic. I'd head back to our place with my pockets bulging and my hands overflowing. Pretty soon I began to walk out to the reef toting a bag or two with the express purpose of collecting the plastic bits and pieces. With bags filled, I'd return to our open-air kitchen and spread the refuse all out on a side table. An amazing array of plastic was lying there before me: lighters, toys, toothbrushes, forks, clothespins, hair barrettes, and on and on. I began to fiddle with plastic pieces, moving them here and there to create little sculptures and assemblages. Out would come the glue if I made a piece that was particularly worthy of saving. That was the beginning of my fascination with creating art with marine debris.

Over the years, I have never stopped picking up plastic. I continue to bring it back to our shack in the sand and create with it. I usually walk the reef in solitude; last year, however, Scooter and I joined a community reef cleanup on World Oceans Day. A small group of volunteers walked together along the reef. We fanned out to make sure we found and picked up every piece of plastic. I followed behind to concentrate on the pieces of microplastic that were so easily missed. When it came time to pitch my bag into Rama's pickup bed, I pulled back from waiting hands. "I want to keep this *pehu* (trash) and make something with it," I told the gang. I was met with blank stares as I tried to explain in my fractured French and limited Tahitian what I had planned.

My normal routine is when I return to our carport after my reef walks, I spread all of the plastic out on our picnic table. The pieces remain there for a day or two to completely dry out. When they're dry, I brush off the sand and seaweed. I also pick up glass, metal, and a variety of colorful nylon ropes. I make separate piles for each category. Within each category,

I sort again by shape, color, and size. When done with sorting, I stand back, visually analyze what I've got to work with, then I ask myself, "What should I make?" Some creations are flat, depicting different types of sea life. Others are just colorful abstract designs. Some pieces are three-dimensional sculptures. In those cases, I use the lazy Susan from our kitchen to turn the piece around and around as I build, making sure each side is balanced in its overall design. I started out using superglue to hold everything in place. I was convinced that was the only thing that could hold it all together. As time has passed, I have discovered that good old white Elmer's glue works just as well. The drying time is a bit longer, but it's a lot cheaper, and my fingertips don't get stuck together.

Each piece I create I give away to friends, neighbors, and acquaintances. A few years back I gave one to Moana and Tarona. They decided to hang it in the Rangiroa city hall where Moana worked for the mayor. The one from the beach cleanup ended up at Rama's house. My next piece will go to our wonderful neighbors, Joa, Charlie, Noam, and Tara. They are the type of people who will appreciate the message in my art.

A few years ago, I was fortunate enough to meet the local art teacher, Nua. She saw my work and asked me to come into her classroom to tell her students about my creations. She projected images of several of my pieces as I explained how I worked and, most importantly, why I picked up plastic off the reef. When I was done with my presentation, the students worked in teams with assorted pieces of *pehu* and glue to make their own marine debris art. It was a fun morning, and I hope the kids learned a little more about why using and discarding plastic has major consequences.

Early on, I began to wonder if other people used marine debris to create art. I googled it and was surprised to see an online group doing exactly what I was doing. The artists are from every corner of the globe. Some of the pieces are incredible. Seeing what others have created has given me inspiration and motivated me to keep going.

About a week ago, I rode my bike over to the reef. I walked and scoured the beach, but I found very little plastic. That is a good sign as far as I am concerned. More good news is that Rangiroa now has a viable recycling program. A few years back, plastic, glass, paper, and aluminum were just carted off to the growing landfill. Now each household has a green recycling bin that is picked up every Wednesday. In addition, another new program encourages people with broken items to bring them in for repair by a small team of MacGyvers who set up once a month at city hall. Their efforts keep more plastic out of the landfill. I read about one lady on a small Caribbean island who took things into her own hands after being disgusted with all the discarded plastic bottles. She set up a factory where all the plastic is melted, extruded, and repurposed into building materials. Now, that is something I would like to see happen here, and, for that matter, all over the world.

One day I hope to be put out of business. I hope there

is zero waste and no more marine debris, and thus nothing for me to pick up along the reef for my creations. Until that day, I will continue making and sharing my art with others.

— *POSTSCRIPT* —

Google "Splashtrash" to see the amazing art created all over the world from plastic detritus by like-minded artists.

TRIP TO MOTU MAHUTA

There are hundreds of *motu* that form the ring creating this vast atoll. We have been to many of them over the years. They are all exceptionally beautiful and wild, each with its own little personality. A few of the many *motu* hold a special place in my heart; Motu Mahuta, however, is my favorite. Yes, it's beautiful, but so are the others. It's the backstory of Mahuta that has held my attention for almost forty years. If you'd care to hear the tale of this special island, grab a cool one, kick off your shoes, and read on.

The year was 1986. I had been to Rangiroa that summer as just one stop on a South Pacific adventure. It was a short stay—only a few days—but it was then that the spell was cast over me. I returned to California in late August after traveling all through Polynesia. Every island I visited was alluring, but it was Rangiroa that was calling me back.

Once home, I immediately bought a Tahiti travel book and flipped directly to the chapter on the Tuamotus and read every detail of the place that I'd experienced so briefly. Under the section in the chapter labeled "Places to Stay," I found a listing under the budget category for a small *pension*, Village Sans Souci. After reading the entry, all I knew for sure was that it was situated on a remote *motu* a one-hour boat ride from Avatoru Village. There was a contact name and a mailing address. There was no email or Internet in those days, so I picked up a pen and put it to paper with my inquiry about a stay.

A plain, white envelope arrived in my Dana Point mailbox more than a month later. Inside was a xeroxed, two-sided brochure with a few fuzzy photos. It included prices and a little description of the setup at Village Sans Souci. It was exactly what I was looking for.

I talked to Chip, my boyfriend at the time, about the atoll adventure. He had come with me the previous summer to experience Bora Bora when I was there for a two-week stop on my big South Pacific journey. He was an ocean guy and anything with saltwater, sand, and sun was right up his alley. We flew out of LAX, then caught the first Air Tahiti flight to Rangiroa the following morning. The view upon approaching the atoll from above was jaw-dropping. Everyone on the plane oohed out loud, and cameras were clicking away as we flew above the immense and beautiful work of nature in all its turquoise magnificence. I looked down and could only wonder where in this vast water wonderland was Village Sans Souci.

As arranged, Gary, the owner of Village Sans Souci, met us at the small airport. An expat American, he had sandy brown hair and was about six feet tall with a muscular build. He had a friendly, easy way about him. We walked across the road to the airport dock and jumped in his skiff. Our first stop was a few minutes up the lagoon in Avatoru Village. After he tied up, we took a short walk to the tiny local store, Magasin Daniel. Constructed of cinder blocks, it was no more than twenty by twenty feet. Meager stores lined the shelves. Gary grabbed an empty cardboard box to use as his shopping cart, then proceeded to walk around selecting his *motu* supplies.

After about an hour heading west in the lagoon, Gary finally slowed down, then turned right into the shallows. He pulled off some slick maneuvering through several large coral heads, and suddenly we were there. We landed on a brilliant white beach. There were about a dozen small *fares* scattered along the shore. Each *fare* featured an A-frame design topped off with a steep, woven thatch roof. Small lanais fronting each *fare*, constructed of native hardwood branches, stood out over the lapping lagoon. There was a larger, main *fare* in the middle of the village where simple meals were prepared. Guests ate breakfast and dinner together on long, wooden tables. A semicold Hinano or Coke could be found for purchase in an ice chest behind the counter that separated the grill from the dining area. The floor was soft, white sand, and the walls were woven from palm fronds. A few handmade decorations adorned the gathering place, and a low panel of traditional Tahitian windows opened toward the lagoon. One corner of the building had a shelf with several books and, just below, a chess board sat ready for players. Everything was so natural, so beautiful, and so quiet. Behind the row of guest *fares* was a large cement shower house. The words *VAHINE* and *TANE* painted in bold, block letters indicated the men's and women's areas. The overhead water system was a Rube Goldberg contraption that provided rainwater to the showers and toilets. Gary and his wife, Nan, had a more substantial home tucked back in thick palms, a discreet distance from the communal areas.

Gary was from Newport Beach. He had been in Tahiti for several years, working in the construction business. Nan had previously worked at a veterinary clinic in Costa Mesa, California. Gary must have had some serious financial backing to be able to build a small *pension* on a remote *motu* in the middle of the South Pacific. He also must have had some sort of pull to be granted permission to lease the *motu*, obtain business approval, and to receive clearance from immigration to continue to live and work in French Polynesia.

I was curious how Village Sans Souci came to be. I asked Gary about it, and he told me his story. He had gathered a group of local men, and together they had hand-cleared the *motu* with razor-sharp machetes. They then built the structures with hammers, saws, and nails, using tree branches for the framework. The thatch roofs were woven with palm fronds, then nailed onto wooden slats in the framed roof. There was a bit of infrastructure he had to deal with, and then there was that ingenious shower house. Thinking about this and knowing what I do today about *motu* life, creating Village Sans Souci had to have been a massive undertaking and a testament to Gary's tenacity and vision.

Gary ran the show, transferred guests to and from the airport, and did all the shopping in the village. He was gregarious and spoke Tahitian to the locals. Nan, on the other hand, although very friendly and warm, never left the *motu*. When we met her, she had not been to the village for five years. What amazed me even more was that she was up to date on worldwide current events. When I asked her about this, she told me she sat up late every night and tuned in to the international news broadcasts with her shortwave radio. With her radio and *motu,* she was as happy as a clam.

The languid passing of our days in this village mentally confirmed what I already instinctively knew: I was meant for *motu* life. It was the rainy season, and we got dumped on for days. In between the squalls, Chip and I took long morning runs along open stretches of sand, collected shells, swam in the warm, crystal-clear lagoon, and explored Mahuta and the neighboring *motu*. We walked the beach as far as we could go in both directions, feeling free, totally alive, and natural.

There were a few other guests at Village Sans Souci. One was a honeymoon couple from Philadelphia. They appeared to be miserable. They would probably have loved the setup better at Club Med Mo'orea with its evening shows, ping pong tables, and organized activities. Another guest, a petite French woman from Avatoru, was perfectly content all by herself. She spent every day, all day, combing the various sand pockets for highly prized miniature shells. She had thousands of pink beauties in a glass liter Coke bottle upon her departure.

We seemed to naturally gravitate toward Gary and Nan. We were close in age, all from Orange County, and had a lot in common. Gary helped me with my Tahitian, and Nan showed me how she cooked freshly caught fish. Just before we were about to depart, Gary took me aside and asked, "Would you be interested in buying Village San Souci?" He explained that it was going up for sale soon and added that he and Nan would be moving on. I stopped dead in my tracks. Of course, I'd love to buy Village Sans Souci. I was already in love with Rangiroa and *motu* life. Living there would be a dream come true. Within seconds of his question, my heart raced, then, just as quickly, it sank. I could never afford to buy such a place. I was on a teacher's salary, and buying little islands in the middle of the South Pacific just wasn't in the budget. For months after that conversation with Gary, I tried to twist and turn my finances every which way, looking for a solution. I even asked my dad to go in with me. Thinking he'd jump at the chance to return to his beloved Tahiti, I was surprised when he just smiled and said, "No." He knew better.

As time passed, I thought often about "my" *motu,* and sometimes I imagined myself out there. In my daydreams, I'd be running back and forth to the village in the skiff, catching fish to cook, picking up supplies at Magasin Daniel, making friends with the locals, and speaking perfect Tahitian.

Over many years, I kept an ear to the coconut wireless, hoping for some news of Motu Mahuta and Village Sans Souci. Finally, one day a friend in Bora Bora told me that Gary and Nan had moved to Mo'orea and that an American couple had bought it. I became obsessed with that couple. Who were they? Where did they come from? How were they doing out there? Did they love atoll life as much as I did? Just the thought of them in "my" imagined home made me envious beyond belief.

Knowing what I do now about *motu* life has made me revise my thoughts about that couple. I now know they were working nonstop not only to survive, but to be able to welcome guests and provide a modicum of comfort in a remote and challenging locale. My envy turned to downright respect as I thought about a couple brave enough to take the leap and make a go of it on a beautiful speck of sand in the middle of nowhere.

From that point on when on the coconut wireless, I never failed to ask if there was any news of the American couple at Village Sans Souci. I was shocked and saddened one day when I heard that there had been a tragedy out there. The husband, trying to save a guest from drowning, had been swept through a swiftly running *hoa* into the open ocean. He was never seen again. The wife stayed on and forged ahead, running Village Sans Souci all alone. My broken heart went out to her. I couldn't imagine the strength that must have taken. I hoped to meet her one day. All that I knew for sure was that her name was Scarlett.

Years later, while in Rangiroa, I asked around about Scarlett. I heard she had gotten married to a local *tane*, moved back to the village, and worked in the back office at Magasin Daniel. The next morning, I rode my bike into Avatoru, approached the *vahine* at the checkout counter, and asked for Scarlett. I was directed to a small office down a short ramp back by the vegetable cooler. After years of wondering about her, suddenly there she was. She was tall and slender with soft brown eyes. Her brown hair was sun-streaked and up in a ponytail. She had a huge, beautiful smile and genuinely welcomed me into her office. We spoke briefly, then agreed to meet up later at her house on the pass when we could sit down and talk.

A day or so later, I followed her directions and found her house. We pulled our chairs up to her big table and began to get to know each other. I told her of my long-ago dream of buying Motu Mahuta and of following her story over the years. She told me of her life on the *motu*. It's a roller-coaster ride of a tale with many over-the-top challenges, strong friendships, and the ever-present help of many people. She told me of surviving a hurricane, learning to navigate Paumotu life, and learning to speak French on the fly. She also told me of meeting Rich, her husband, who had come out to help her with the cooking. She had found love again and was leading a truly blessed life. She and Rich had moved to the village a few years prior. She had a thriving business teaching English and piano. Everyone knows and loves her. We became fast friends.

Fast forward to about a year ago. I had been wanting to go back to Motu Mahuta, just to check it out. Having Scarlett and Rich along would be fun and helpful if we were going to find the *motu* and secure a safe anchorage. We decided to wait for favorable weather and then make the journey. I had not been there since the 1980s. Scarlett and Rich had been out for a picnic a few years prior. Scooter had only just heard about the place.

On a calm day, the four of us packed up a picnic and headed out. Entry to Mahuta is challenging because the sand flats are vast and shallow. We got only so far before it became too shallow to navigate in *Vahine Iti*, so we anchored the boat and continued on foot through the ankle-deep saltwater. Along the walk, we stopped at a neighboring *motu* and met a friendly family there. Finally, at Mahuta, we began to slowly survey the place. To be there with Scarlett and Rich was unbelievable. They knew every nook and cranny of the *motu* and could decipher what we were looking at as we explored, despite the changes wrought by the intervening years. There was a pad of sorts where the kitchen had been, and a part of the old stove was lying on the ground. Other than that, the main building was totally gone. Palm fronds, coconuts, and sand littered the ground where once there had been tables, chairs, a bookcase, and a chess board. No guest *fares* still stood; however, remnants of the massive shower house could be seen among the tangled vines. Everything had gone back to nature, and Village Sans Souci was just a memory. Nevertheless, Mahuta holds a lure for me. It always will. Even though Village Sans Souci is gone, the best part of the story is that it led me to Scarlett, who has become my very best friend in all of French Polynesia.

— *POSTSCRIPT* —

I never heard another word about Gary and Nan. I have tried to locate them over the years, with no luck whatsoever. I still have the Village San Souci brochure that Gary snail mailed me way back in the mid-1980s.

Mahuta *means "flock of birds suddenly rising up" in Tahitian. There are several Motu Mahutas in Rangiroa, though I'm not sure why.*

Sans Souci *means "without a care" in French. What a perfect name for that special, magical place.*

MEETING JILLYN

I am fascinated with the concept of doppelgängers—finding two unrelated people who look like twins. I have met my doppelgänger. Sherry lived in Dana Point when I did and was a lifeguard at Doheny State Beach. I never saw her, met her, or knew anything about her at the time. She knew about me, though. I used to run the streets of the harbor every morning. People kept telling Sherry, "I saw you running this morning." It wasn't where she had been, so she knew something was up. Finally, she spotted me and instantly figured it all out.

Fast forward several years to the aisles of KTA, my preferred grocery store in Kona. I was happily minding my own business when Sherry came down the same aisle in the opposite direction. I was busy picking up a can of enchilada sauce, oblivious to my fellow shoppers. As I meandered down the aisle with my cart, I suddenly heard a loud voice directed at me say, "It's YOU again!" I looked up to see my twin. Right then and there, Sherry told me about all the mix-ups back in

Dana Point. By complete coincidence, we had both moved to Kona. "Here we go again," Sherry muttered. We were the same height and build. We both had very long, blond hair. Our eye color matched, and our faces were eerily similar. To make it more confusing, she was a boat captain in Honokohau Harbor, Scooter's domain. If that wasn't enough, I ended up buying her beautiful old Range Rover. We got a good laugh out of being twins and had fun confusing everyone we collectively knew. A few years later, Sherry moved on to another captain's gig in the Caribbean. I was on my own again.

Meeting Sherry was a crazy experience. Meeting Jillyn was a whole different ball game. Meeting Jillyn stopped me dead in my tracks. Here's the story of another type of doppelgänger, one who shares your life story. If you have a little time to spare, read on to hear the tale of Carol and Jillyn.

All over French Polynesia, I have met many fellow travelers. Most are in Tahiti just briefly, only to move on to the next destination on their bucket list. Some people really love Tahiti. They have found their special island, their special place to stay, and they have fostered long-running friendships with their special Tahitian friends. These people return like clockwork once each year. A few people are like me: steadfast Tahiti Nuts. We are the people who aren't content to come for a two-week holiday. We aren't happy coming once a year. We want to hunker down and live the Tahitian way and stretch our stay to the maximum allowable days set by immigration. We want to walk, talk, dance, sing, eat, breathe, and infuse everything Polynesian into our souls and keep it right there forever. We go to extremes to get here and stay here. Nothing else will do. Nothing will get in our way. When we are not in Tahiti, we think about our adopted homeland incessantly. We cry when longing for the place, sing along with Tahitian songs on our playlists, and keep careful track on the calendar of how many days remain until we get to board that flight and turn south. Now that I have written the above definition of a Tahiti Nut, I honestly can't think of anyone I've met who is in the same category as me, except Jillyn.

A few years back I never knew Jillyn existed. I thought that maybe I was the only person in the world who had my stage of the Tahiti Disease. That all changed one day when I got a call from my pal, Smitty. She had been to a vintage woodie (wood-paneled station wagons highly prized in the surf world) show in Dana Point Harbor. Circling the spotless classic cars were various vendors under pop-up canopies. Smitty noticed a booth with beautiful silver and black pearl jewelry utilizing Polynesian motifs. She briefly spoke with the artist, picked up one of the displayed business cards, and immediately thought of me. When Smitty called, she gave me the contact information for Moni Tapu, Jillyn's jewelry line. When I pulled up her website, I froze in place. Her line was extraordinarily stunning, but it was the backstory that had me riveted to my computer screen. Jillyn's dad and his passion for Polynesia were the inspiration for her bold designs cast in silver. Black-and-white photos of a man that reminded me of my dad were integrated seamlessly into her website.

After carefully perusing every detail of her site, I sent her an email introducing myself. She replied promptly, then we proceeded to email back and forth in a crazed frenzy. Next, we moved to the telephone. We spoke for hours and compared the many and various details of our respective lives. Both of us were amazed at all of the similarities in our backgrounds.

Jillyn's dad was a US Marine pilot stationed on Ulithi Atoll in the Caroline Islands during the entirety of World War II. His wartime experience in the South Pacific was the beginning of his lifelong love affair with Polynesia. The montage of photos I saw on her website showed a man on his atoll with a smile on his face, war or no war.

My dad was stationed in Hawaii at Pearl Harbor during WWII. Yes, the war was raging, and he had serious duties as a naval officer; however, being in Hawaii fulfilled a childhood dream. He had always wanted to see the South Pacific, gleaning his inspiration from the many tales of the South Seas he had read in the icy cold winters of Rhode Island. In the dark of night, he smelled the sweet scent of flowers upon his approach to Hawaii aboard his naval transport vessel. He fell in love with the islands right then and there on the deck of his warship. It was a love affair that would last until his final days.

Both of our fathers were engineers. My dad specialized in aerospace and worked at North American Aviation, helping develop technology used in early space exploration. Jillyn's dad worked as an electrical engineer for Pacific Bell Telephone. He designed where trunk and cable lines would be placed.

The big news in 1961 for both of our dads was that direct flights from LAX to the recently completed runway at Fa'a'a in Tahiti were about to commence. My parents wasted no time after learning this, and in May of that year, they climbed aboard the inaugural flight of TAI Airlines. The plane turned south, and they were off on the adventure of a lifetime. Jillyn's parents were right behind them as they took off a year later in the spring of 1962.

Both sets of parents were fortunate enough to experience Tahiti as it was then: unspoiled, natural, wide open, and, dare I say, innocent. They met many incredibly vibrant local characters. They both trekked to Mo'orea and Bora Bora, not an easy task in those days. They both met the infamous Bali Hai Boys, and both were asked if they'd care to join in with the fledgling hotel. Both sets of parents returned to California with Eddie Lund LPs, custom clothes made at Marie Ah You, then proceeded to keep the magic alive by hosting Polynesian *tama'ara'as* with like-minded friends and visiting Tahitians. It was at those glorious backyard parties that Jillyn and I both got bitten by the Tahiti bug.

Jillyn's dad took it one step further than my dad. He promised Jillyn that if she learned to dance Tahitian, he'd take her on his next trip to Tahiti. Jillyn found a dance troupe and began to dance. Little did her dad know that Tahitian dance would become her lifelong passion. She ended up dancing professionally in the LA area and also learned to play the Tahitian *uturere*. Jillyn's dad made good on that promise and took her on her first trip to Tahiti in 1979.

I sure wish my dad had tried that little tactic with me. I had to wait until I was an adult to begin my travels to the South Pacific. Even though I had to wait, Dad and I got to share time together when he rented a cool little house on Motu To'opua when I was living in Bora Bora during the summer of 1987.

While Jillyn was dancing the *tamure* and strumming her *uturere,* I became passionate about learning to speak Tahitian. I had taken two years of French in high school and detested every minute of it. I knew passable Spanish, a remnant of my many trips to Mexico over the years. That language didn't interest me much either. With Tahitian, I couldn't get enough. I devoured everything I could find to help me improve. I met and made friends with the head professor of Indo-Pacific languages at the University of Hawaii. He kindly helped me over the years, one on one. I have several Tahitian language dictionaries and have read them all cover to cover many times while highlighting new words and making notes in the margins. I even have a pirated Tahitian study guide from the Mormon Missionary Training Center, which is generally regarded as the pinnacle of language acquisition institutions. That guided lesson workbook is now completely worn out and dog-eared, but I know sentence structure, how to change tenses, all the various pronouns, and most of the other language intricacies. Over many years, I made flash cards of every word and phrase I learned. I filed each three-by-five-inch index card alphabetically in a small box. That small box had to morph into increasingly larger boxes as I acquired more words. I listened to audios, translated song lyrics, and read epic Tahitian poetry, hoping to bolster my knowledge. After all is said and done, I've decided that living here in Rangiroa and speaking Tahitian as often as I can is really the best way to improve.

I have three siblings; Jillyn has one older sister. For some reason, only Jillyn and I out of our families got infected with the Tahiti Disease. Neither one of us is sure why. Jillyn's daughter picked up the baton of Tahitian dance and carried the torch onward for her family.

Jillyn's mom and my mom were along for the exotic ride with no complaints whatsoever. Both moms were happy about being a part of the alluring adventures, though I believe it was our dads who gave us the disease.

Jillyn married Dane, who jumped right into the Polynesian program. Scooter did the same. Jillyn and I were both very lucky in that department.

Meeting Jillyn was a miracle. In this big, wide world, we managed to cross paths. At first, our friendship was conducted over the Internet and phone. We tried to meet when we were both in Pape'ete a few years back. The timing wasn't right. Even though we were in the same town at the same time, Scooter and I had a flight to catch, and we couldn't connect with Jillyn and Dane. A few years after that, Jillyn and Dane were aboard the *Aranui,* returning from the Marquesas. The *Aranui* usually pulls in here every ten days; unfortunately, on that particular voyage, it was bypassing Rangiroa and stopping in at Makatea, a neighboring atoll. Once again, we were so close, yet so far. As fate would have it, a storm arrived just as the *Aranui* approached the Tuamotus. The stop at Makatea would be too dangerous; suddenly, there was a change of plans. It looked like the *Aranui* would be coming to Rangiroa after all. What luck! Jillyn emailed me the news from her cabin, and we got ready for a visit from my doppelgänger Tahiti twin.

I met Jillyn and Dane as they arrived, took them on the nickel tour, then brought them home to meet Scooter. It was a blustery and rainy day, so they weren't treated to the sparkling, turquoise lagoon we had hoped to show them in *Vahine Iti.* Nevertheless, we finally met, and it was just about perfect. Meeting her gave me the same feeling that I have when I'm with my siblings and longtime friends—nothing needs to be explained. We just get each other.

DON'T CRY

"Don't cry because it's over.
Smile because it happened."
—***DR. SEUSS***

Our five-year lease is coming to an end in a few months. Moana and Tarona have agreed to let us extend our time by one or two more years. We are going to see how things go and if we are still physically able to continue. Our original plan was to get enough of Rangiroa so we could move past atoll life and on to other adventures. It seems as if the five-year plan has backfired on us. We're just not ready to pack it in yet. If anything, we have come to love it here more than ever. Moving on from this place has been heavy on my mind. Normally I don't dwell on things, especially things that I know are inevitable. In this case, I can't help but dread our final goodbye, even if it's still two years off in the future.

I've been mentally formulating what the essence of this

experience boils down to. Why don't you pour yourself one last cold one and read on to find out what we will take away when we finally do move out of our beloved shack in the sand?

There's just something about the pace of life here that feels so natural. Yes, we plan, but mostly things are done spontaneously. Feel like fishing? Grab the poles and bring the boat from the *hoa*. Let's go! Need some beer for an impromptu gathering on the lanai? A quick trip on the e-bike to Magasin Vaimariu—the closest store—will fill the fridge with some Hinanos, pronto. Need to see the doctor? No appointment needs to be made weeks in advance. Just peddle to the clinic and wait your turn under the cool shade of the trees. Want to go on a sunset cruise to check out the new yachts? Drop the rake, take off those gardening gloves, and grab your rum drink and a tin of cocktail peanuts. Yahoo!

There's something about living mostly outside. It feels good. We're so much more in tune with . . . LIFE! All day, every day, we witness a parade of fish, birds, John Ford clouds, all types of boats, and sleek Polynesian canoes. We've come to know most of the local boats, their respective crews, and many of the paddlers. We wave *'iaorana* to them as they pass by just a few yards out front. We watch the mega yachts loaded down with all the big boy toys just as carefully as we watch the (sometimes) ragtag sailboats pull in to anchor.

Everything we see sparks our interest. One morning, a few weeks ago, we saw a solo dolphin arch up in a high, beautiful leap just as we were taking a bite of our morning toast. It's only the second time we've seen a dolphin inside the lagoon. Living within the realm of nature's elements never gets old, and it is definitely better than Netflix.

There's something about being a guest in a foreign culture that always makes you want to put your best foot forward. We are but two insignificant ambassadors from the US. We strive to leave good impressions. Americans are generally well-received here, and we have been fortunate enough to be on the receiving end of some warm aloha. We've all seen the too-pushy, me-first, entitled traveler who is an embarrassment to his or her home country. We hope to always put a positive spin on what Americans can, and should, be.

There's something about the people. The population is a mishmash of French and Polynesian. The two diametrically opposed cultures have managed to blend into a concoction of humanity that's just about perfect. We've met incredibly wonderful people. Most are casual acquaintances; many are solid friends; others have become *feti'i*, family. Living on an atoll removes all the fluff. You're left with down to earth individuals all living together in a challenging locale. People readily share and are quick to help each other. Our setup at Moana's Village is so much more communal than what we had been used to. The current combination of occupants in our little community of four houses works seamlessly, and we all have fun. It was an adjustment for us, but we're finding it's nice to share space with great people. Overall, we feel as if we have become a very small part of this atoll's society. Families are large, and people are interconnected through marriage or blood. Histories and relationships go back generations. We honor and respect this ongoing culture that is deep, complicated, and proud. We're not sure how we fit in, but it feels like we do.

Living in a place where supplies are limited has made us more efficient and creative. We somehow find what we need and never waste anything. Ever. We've had so much fun figuring out ways to make do with what we've got on hand. I've never been an overconsumer or waster, but now I'm even more streamlined. It's also given us a deeper appreciation for the abundance in America.

We have worked hard on our house to slowly build a home that is comfortable and inviting. Tarona was just here from Pape'ete this past weekend. We stood together on the beach and looked back at the house and yard. "You've built your own little paradise," she whispered to me. Five years ago, she and Moana put their faith in us to care for their beautiful property. It has been an honor to live here and an honor to care for it.

We have learned so much, and we continue to learn. Just this morning, Scooter said, "I learned something new yesterday." I was curious about what else we could possibly learn. He told me he saw Meho making herself a cool drink and watched as she plopped ice cubes that she had made in a muffin tin into her cup. That's a great idea. Ice melts so quickly here. The larger cubes last longer. I'm going to do that, too.

Besides large, slow-melting ice cubes, we have learned how to get fresh food and everyday supplies, how to figure out the cargo ship schedules, and how to fish in these waters. We have learned some French and even more Tahitian. We have learned to prepare new foods and build a barbecue fire using coconut husks. We learned new songs, which we sang with joy, and danced the *tamure* to the pulse of the *to'ere* drums. I have learned to hang laundry efficiently and how to read the approaching clouds as a vital part of the drying process. We have learned about kilometers, liters, kilograms, and using Tahitian French francs. We have come to partially understand the offbeat Polynesian humor. We have learned about trees, plants, and flowers, and what can be made with them. The list goes on and on.

There's something about the natural beauty of an atoll. In my mind, it's akin to an additional natural wonder of the world. I hope everybody gets the chance to experience this mind-boggling beauty at least once in their lives. What I've been fortunate enough to see with my own two eyes never ceases to amaze me. In this crazy, fast-paced world, there are still miles and miles of open land on hundreds of picturesque *motu*, millions of palm trees, empty white sand beaches, and brilliant turquoise water. I want to breathe it all in forever.

Just now, something crazy happened. I put my iPad on hold, put on my sunnies and trusty Crocs, and walked out to the edge of the lagoon. A fancy inflatable tender pulled right up to our beach with seven or eight people on board.

They had good rock music playing and looked like they were ready to party. I asked Scooter, "Are we expecting anyone?" I looked back at the kitchen table to see him shake his head. It turns out the merrymakers were from one of the yachts moored in the lagoon. They had passed by a bit earlier and thought our place was a bar. They returned with a boatload of friends, ready to be served some *maita'is*. I do have a lot of colorful chairs and tables all over, so I could see how the mistake could have been made. We all had a good laugh, said our hellos in several languages and our goodbyes in several other languages, and off they went. It's stuff like that that seems to happen here. It's never dull. That's for sure.

This stay has had its fair share of drama. Not the good kind. It started out with a huge snafu upon arrival at immigration in Pape'ete. The scare of a lifetime left us both quaking as we sat sequestered inside the glass booth with all our fellow Hawaiian Airlines passengers looking at us and wondering if we were drug runners. Over the course of a week and with a lot of help from longtime friends, it all got straightened out. That experience is something we hope to never repeat. Next up, I had a bad fall on the *feo* (sharp coral) as I got out from a swim. My injuries were serious. That afternoon I could be found at the clinic getting stitches and having both legs wrapped in mummy-like dressings. Instead of running, walking, swimming, diving, and fishing, I was meeting every day with the community outreach nurse. She arrived every morning for fifteen days to check my wounds, watch the progress of my stitches, and redress me with a white, stretchy wrap. My daily saltwater fix was shelved for a month while I healed. If that wasn't enough, while I was still shuffling around with two bandaged legs, Scooter came down with shingles. At first, we thought it was an allergic reaction to a wasp sting on his forehead. After three trips to the two atoll doctors, the diagnosis was finally made. I did all I could to make him comfortable. It was brutal. I thought that I was going to lose him one particularly long, scary night. I stood over the bed looking at him and asked myself, "What the heck are we doing in a place so remote with limited medical support at our age?" I felt so helpless. It made us both realize how things can change in a heartbeat. One minute all is rosy and bright. The next minute all the fun and normalcy get tossed out the window, and we're flat on our backs in pain.

We are leaving on Saturday. Today, we are slowly packing up. We'll pull the boat and mooring out of the lagoon this afternoon with the help of Teiva and Meho. We've gotten pretty good at this closing-down routine. Each of us goes about our respective tasks silently and efficiently, mentally checking off everything that needs to get done. We'll be back in three months, lugging four maxed-out suitcases, two heavy carry-ons, and two impossibly overstuffed backpacks. It will take several days to do the reverse of today's tasks to open everything back up again. After that's done, we'll settle back in to enjoy more of what atoll life has to offer. And, in the very end, when we are finally ready to move on for good, I will do my best to follow the suggestion of good old Dr. Seuss: I will not cry because it's over. I will smile because it happened.

— POSTSCRIPT —

I have enjoyed writing my atoll stories. I began writing because so many people have asked me questions about our lives here. Everyone wondered what could possibly take us away from Hawaii. Now you know.

ACKNOWLEDGMENTS

There are many people that helped me publish *Sand, Sea, and Sky*, to whom I am grateful. A brief selection of those people are

- CarolLyn Sakata, Eva Hillman, and Cheryl Quimby Stevenson for their technical support
- Stephen Cline for his publishing guidance
- Sarah Lee for her gorgeous underwater photography
- Ron Haake for his photographic expertise, and
- Gillian Barth for her editing guidance

ABOUT THE AUTHOR

Carol Fuller, originally from Southern California, has spent much of her life in the South Pacific. She currently lives in Holualoa on the lush slopes above Kailua-Kona, Hawaii. A member of the Salt Water Tribe, her days revolve around the tides and waves. *Sand, Sea, and Sky* is her first published memoir about life in Tahiti.

sandseaandskybook@gmail.com